KU-013-077

Contents

Making Sense of the Private Finance Initiative

developing public–private partnerships

Courtney A Smith

Economic Adviser
NHS Executive

Foreword by

Hadyn Cook

Chief Executive
Calderdale NHS Trust

RADCLIFFE MEDICAL PRESS

Radcliffe Medical Press
18 Marcham Road, Abingdon, Oxon OX14 1AA

British Library Cataloguing in Publication Data

A catalogue record for this book is available from the British Library.

ISBN 1 85775 381 X

Typeset by Joshua Associates Ltd, Oxford
Printed and bound by TJ International Ltd, Padstow, Cornwall

Foreword

The private finance initiative has revolutionised the way the public sector procures the facilities that it requires to deliver modern public services. The policy is now gathering pace across the various parts of the public sector and is likely to remain an integral part of the government's modernisation programme for the 21st century.

The publication of *Making Sense of the Private Finance Initiative: developing public–private partnerships* is timely. As the policy approaches its seventh anniversary, there is a need to take stock of the lessons learnt, record best practice, clarify key principles, and consider options for further improving the PFI process and product. Those who are newcomers to the PFI scene or who are not *au fait* with what is entailed in conducting a successful PFI procurement, will find Dr Smith's book to be an indispensable resource. Public sector and private sector bodies, including their advisers, no longer need to waste money and time re-inventing wheels and going down blind alleys. Written mainly from a financial perspective, the book provides advice and practical tips on all aspects of the business case and procurement process. It also contains two detailed case studies of *real PFI schemes* – the procurement of a new hospital at Calderdale NHS Trust and information technology services at Liverpool Women's Hospital. The author's considerable experience in advising on PFI procurements is reflected in each of the nine lucidly written chapters. He has succeeded in demystifying the policy without distorting the realities of what PFI entails in practice.

My only regret is that such a book was not available at the time my Trust was undertaking its PFI procurement. It would have certainly helped to reduce the length and costs of the procurement and the frustrations encountered in the process. It would also have helped us to understand the approval criteria for the business case and what information to include in the submission. The lack of detailed guidance on a number of key issues and generic problems, such as accounting treatment and vires of NHS organisations to enter into PFI contracts, were major sources of frustration for our project team and private sector partners.

PFI has proved to be an effective policy for harnessing private sector capital and expertise to deliver government objectives, at the same time as conferring benefits on the private sector. As the private sector and public sector become more accustomed to working together, value for money for the taxpayer will continue to improve. More innovative deals will also be negotiated. There is also the prospect of exporting the policy to developing and developed countries alike in the same way as the UK has exported market testing and privatisation.

Hadyn Cook
Chief Executive of Calderdale NHS Trust
June 1999

About the author

Dr Courtney Smith holds degrees in economics from University of Manchester, University of Hull, University of the West Indies (Jamaica) and University of Tromso (Norway). He has held various posts in the Government Economic Service over the past 11 years, including Economic Adviser on PFI/PPP and capital investment issues in the NHS Executive. He is currently Economic Adviser to the NHS Information Authority. His other publications include *Socialist Transformation in Peripheral Economies*, Avebury Press, Aldershot, 1995.

Acknowledgements

This book would not have been possible without the support and helpful comments from a large number of people. I am grateful to all of them.

Among those who deserve special mention are Clive Smee (Chief Economic Adviser in the Department of Health), Jeremy Hurst, Ray Blundell, Peter Coates, Peter Cockett, Lenora Clarke, Stephen Dunn, Ayesha Dost, David Revell, Ralph Lewars, Calvin McDonald, Levi Atkinson, Enola Beharie, Andrew Lloyd-Kendal, Barbara O'Leary and Carl Vincent.

The contribution of Haydn Cook (lead author of Chapter 7), David Young (lead author of Chapter 8) and Joe Flanagan (contributor to Chapter 9 and lead reviewer) are gratefully appreciated.

Naomi Smith, my daughter, was a major source of inspiration – although only seven years old, she has already learned the virtues of patience and hard work. Arthur and Rosemary Bennett, my parents and other relatives provided much needed moral support. I also owe much to my former tutors and lecturers who have continued to inspire me, particularly Professor Mike Artis, Dr Mark Figueroa, Professor Gavin Mooney, Dr Paul Sutton and Dr Michael Witter.

Last, but certainly not least, I would like to thank my commissioning editor, Gillian Nineham, and the rest of her team, particularly Jamie Etherington, Gregory Moxon and Paula Moran for the high standard of service provided throughout the various stages of the project. Without their professionalism and commitment, the project would have stagnated.

None of the individuals mentioned above nor their organisations are in any way responsible for the views expressed in this book. Responsibility for any errors of omission or commission rests solely with the author.

List of abbreviations

APM	Arbitrage Pricing Model
CAPM	Capital Asset Pricing Model
CBI	Confederation of British Industry
CCN	Change Control Notice
CCP	Change Control Procedure
CCT	compulsory competitive tendering
CDM	construction, design and management
CFO	conventionally funded option
CHC	Community Health Council
CIM	Capital Investment Manual
CPAG	Capital Prioritisation Advisory Group
DBFO	design, build, finance and operate
DSON	detailed statement of need
EAC	equivalent annual cost
ECR	extra-contractual referral
FBC	Full Business Case
FCEs	finished consultant episodes
GIGO	garbage in garbage out
HImP	Health Improvement Programme
HISS	hospital information support system
IfH	Information for Health
IM&T	information management and technology
IS/IT	information services and technology
ITN	Invitation to Negotiate
ITT	Invitation to Tender
LAN	local area network
NAO	National Audit Office
NPC	net present cost
NPV	net present value
OBC	Outline Business Case
OBS	output-based specification
OJEC	Official Journal of the European Community
PCG	primary care group
PFI	Private Finance Initiative
PFU	private finance unit
PPP	public/private partnership
PRINCE	PRojects IN a Controlled Environment
PSC	public sector comparator
RAM	risk allocation matrix

RPI	retail price index
SMART	specific, measurable, achievable, relevant and time-constrained
SOC	Strategic Outline Case
SON	statement of need
SPV	special purpose vehicle
TSC	Technical Sub-Committee
TUPE	Transfer of Undertakings (Protection of Employment) Regulations 1981
WAN	wide area network

List of figures

To Naomi, Barbara, Evelyn, Monica and the
memory of Robin

Introduction

Since 1979, successive governments in the United Kingdom have introduced a range of private sector initiatives designed to improve the provision of public services. The Private Finance Initiative (PFI), launched in autumn 1992 by the then Chancellor of the Exchequer, Norman Lamont, is the latest in this series of measures. Previous initiatives include privatisation, compulsory competitive tendering, market testing and the creation of Next Steps Agencies.

PFI has now become the *dominant method* for procuring the facilities to deliver services within government departments, local authorities and other semi-autonomous bodies in the UK. Since May 1997, the new Labour administration has also adopted the policy and is vigorously promoting PFI and developing other models of public/private partnerships (PPP). The underlying rationale for the policy has remained the same. It seeks to provide improved and more cost-effective services to the public using the combined resources and skills of the public and private sectors. It is not merely about involving the private sector in the financing of capital projects in the public sector, but also about harnessing the full range of private sector management, commercial and creative skills in the design, build and operation of capital schemes.

As a method of procuring public services, the appeal of the policy is in no way restricted to the UK public sector. Suitably adapted, PFI can be applied to the procurement of public services in developing and developed countries alike. Governments throughout the world face the same age-old challenge to deliver their objectives in a way that makes effective use of all available resources, whether owned by the public or private sector. Where the use of private finance and the harnessing of the private sector's management skills can deliver better value for money than the publicly funded alternative, there is no cost-benefit justification for pursuing the latter course.

Although PFI is now in its seventh year, and despite the widespread interest which it commands, it is surprising just how little serious analysis and informed commentary exist on the subject. Debate on issues such as the potential of PFI to deliver improved value for money to tax-payers abounds but, for the most part, this discourse is conducted at a philosophical level. The general paucity of evaluation evidence and case study material makes it impossible to resolve such controversies. This lacuna also gives rise to a waste of resources as the various parties involved in PFI transactions expend time, money and effort reinventing wheels. This results in longer and more costly procurements.

This book is a direct response to this problem. Drawing on the available evidence, lessons learned to date and the author's considerable experience in advising on PFI procurements, the work is designed to promote understanding of the PFI in the NHS and wider public sector and sharply reduce the gradient of the PFI learning curve. The book has a deliberate *practical* focus aimed at meeting the needs of the various stakeholders involved in PFI procurements. These include policy-makers, project managers, advisers and practitioners at all levels on the public sector side; and the various business sectors involved in PFI provision (construction, engineering and design, service providers, financiers, commercial lawyers, management consultants and other professional advisers). The book is written for both a national and international audience. Those who are undertaking or advising on PFI procurements for the first time will find it invaluable. It is liberally endowed with case studies, good practice tips, checklists, answers to frequently asked questions, pointers to other relevant guidance and information sources, and guidance on the key aspects of the procurement and *business case* development process. Much of the empirical basis for the book derives from the health sector. The NHS has, essentially, been used as a case study to illustrate the opportunities and challenges posed by PFI and PPP arrangements. Where available, secondary evidence has also been drawn from case studies in other sectors, most notably, prisons and transport.

In many respects, the NHS provides an excellent case study for this type of study. It is a major player in the PFI market. It is also worth noting that health is the second largest spending programme of the government after social security, accounting for some 16.7% of spending on public services in the UK in 1996/97 and employing over one million persons.

Despite the jokes about the disappointing experience of PFI in the NHS prior to 1997, arguably, it was a 'training ground' for many other public sector departments. Many of the fundamental PFI principles and much of the practice emerged from this sector. For example, the NHS was the first sector to formalise the requirement to explore private finance to meet capital investment needs where appropriate, reserving public capital provision for those areas where private finance was inappropriate or could not be expected to pass the value-for-money and risk transfer tests. This announcement in November 1993 by the then Parliamentary Under-Secretary of State for Health, Tom Sackville, was generalised by the Chancellor in November 1994. From being one of the most disappointing performers in 1996 (in terms of signed PFI deals), few, if any, would disagree that the NHS has been the best performing area for PFI in 1997 and 1998. This is set to continue in 1999.

The early experience of the NHS illustrates many of the issues arising from the policy: the slow progress of the policy; the difficulty of overcoming financiers' fears; and concerns about the way schemes are selected for PFI testing – length and cost of the procurement process, difficulties of obtaining optimal risks transfer (hence best value for money), affordability, the terms on which staff are transferred as part of a PFI contract, accounting treatment and revenue consequences of long-term contracts. Experience in this sector also throws into sharp relief many of the technical issues posed by PFI proposals, such as construction of public sector comparators, assessment of value for money, risk transfer, affordability and accounting treatment.

Although other sectors can learn from practice in the NHS, it should also be remembered that there are a number of issues which are largely peculiar to this sector. These include the nature of the PFI product (particularly the exclusion of clinical services from private sector contracts), the decentralised structure of NHS organisations, resultant vires issues and the challenge of applying the classical PFI model in the non-acute sector where schemes are small and have a limited service content. Some of these constraints also apply to local government schemes. Caution should therefore be exercised in generalising from the NHS's experience.

The book is comprised of nine chapters. Each chapter is carefully woven with a blend of theoretical and empirical material. In the quest to make the work practical, the balance is tilted towards empirical evidence and best practice tools and techniques.

Chapter 1 traces the evolution of the policy, explains its economic and social rationale, and how it is designed to work. Chapter 2 explains the role of capital in the delivery of healthcare, the nature of the PFI health product, progress of PFI to date in the health sector, the capital investment process and the planning of PFI procurements in the NHS. The experience of the NHS is compared and contrasted with the wider public sector. Chapter 3 outlines the procurement process and how it fits with the business case process. Emphasis is placed on tips for planning and managing the procurement process to maximise the chance of a successful outcome. Chapter 4 examines the importance of risk analysis in PFI transactions. It provides tools and techniques for identifying, assessing, allocating and managing risks. Risk is examined from the perspectives of public sector clients, financiers and service providers. The case for risk-adjusted discount rates and the utility of the Capital Asset Pricing Model is also discussed in this chapter.

Chapter 5 addresses the value for money requirement – the *raison d'être* for the policy. The author analyses the requirements of the three crucial value-for-money decisions which apply to a properly executed procurement: best service solution, best bid and best method of funding. This chapter also discusses public sector comparators and the importance of affordability and solutions for absorbing affordability gaps.

Chapter 6 provides tips for preparing and presenting the business case. It addresses the standard criteria which public watchdog bodies such as the National Audit Office (NAO) and the approval authority would expect PFI projects to satisfy. A five-stage model is presented in this chapter for structuring the contents of the business case. This model, in turn, is linked directly to the approval criteria. The model is one of the many innovations introduced by the author to improve the PFI process. This model is generic and can be readily applied to any sector inside and outside the UK. It reflects best practice.

Chapters 7 and 8 provide two detailed case studies (serviced accommodation for a new hospital with a capital cost of £77 million and a major information technology project) to illustrate the practice of PFI. The hospital case study is largely written by Hadyn Cook, Chief Executive of Calderdale NHS Trust; and the IT case study by David Young, Director of Information Services at Liverpool Women's Hospital NHS Trust. Both case studies provide comprehensive lessons and tips to inform future PFI procurements.

Chapter 9 concludes with a summary of lessons learned to date and some ideas for future development of the policy. The main focus is on ideas for improving the PFI product and, to a lesser extent, the process. The chapter also discusses the prospects for PFI outside the UK.

The views expressed in this work are those of the author and should not be attributed to the Department of Health. It does not represent official guidance. Readers should also note that the book has been produced in the author's own time and has not, in any way, benefited from public resources.

The book is the result of over two years of painstaking research effort and considerable personal sacrifice. Now that the job is done, I look forward to rediscovering my hobbies and rebuilding relationships with friends and relatives, some of whom have been neglected over the gestation period of the work.

CHAPTER ONE

An overview of the policy framework

This chapter sets the scene for the book. It traces the evolution of PFI and the public expenditure context into which the policy was introduced. It also examines the objectives, principles and workings of the policy. It is worth noting from the outset that PFI was introduced by way of government public policy rather than by statute. As we will see, this helps to explain a number of the difficulties which beset the policy in the early stages of its implementation, particularly the old chesnut of ultra vires.

Background

The role of the public sector in the United Kingdom and many other northern economies has been rolled back over the past two decades as part of the quest to improve value for money and stimulate economic growth. The UK has been at the forefront of these changes, as evidenced by the introduction of policies such as compulsory competitive tendering (CCT), market testing, and the large-scale privatisation of the telecommunications, energy, water and transport sectors in the 1980s. Equally far-reaching has been the establishment of 'executive agencies' which separates the institution setting policy from the organisation which undertakes that policy. In many instances, this idea has been extended to giving the private sector direct responsibility to provide services traditionally delivered by the public sector in an explicit contracting-out relationship (Corry 1997).

The introduction of private finance under the aegis of the Private Finance Initiative (PFI) in 1992 is the latest in this series of measures aimed at improving the way public services are delivered in the UK. As Heald (1996, p. 160) argues, 'The Government has sought to identify in the PFI an extension of the privatisation policies which it judges to have been so successful in the formerly nationalised sector'. The current government may not fully share these sentiments but it is keen to build on this success and realise the potential for better value for money through the use of a wide spectrum of partnerships that combine public and private sector skills and resources. The policy represents a major breakthrough and is now firmly embedded in the procurement culture of public sector organisations.

Key objectives and principles

Launched in autumn 1992 by the then Chancellor of the Exchequer, Norman Lamont, PFI has now become the *dominant method* in the UK for procuring public services within government departments and the wider public sector, including the NHS and local authorities.

The objectives of PFI are implicit in the following statement from Kenneth Clarke in November 1993:

> We aim to promote efficiency, to improve services and to stimulate fresh flows of investment. We want to harness the private sector's management expertise and resources, bringing a new approach to investment in a whole range of activities and services traditionally regarded as the exclusive domain of the public sector.

In November 1997, Gordon Brown, Chancellor under the new Labour administration, restated the objectives with the same enthusiasm:

> Through the Private Finance Initiative, the private sector is able to bring a wide range of managerial, commercial and creative skills to the provision of public services, offering potentially huge benefits to the Government (Treasury Task-force November 1997, p. i).

The underlying objective is thus to secure improved value for money to the public sector in the procurement of services. One way of achieving this outcome is to apportion risk optimally between the public and private sectors. This is often cited as the second objective of PFI. Each party is expected to assume the risks which they are best placed to manage, whether by reducing the probability of its occurrence or its likely financial consequences, or both. This 'risk transfer' objective is closely bound up with the 'value-for-money' objective. Inappropriate risk transfer to the private sector will undermine value for money since the private sector, assumed to be rational economic agents, will charge a premium for assuming risks which are traditionally borne by the public sector.

It is important to note that PFI shifts the emphasis from the procurement of *assets* to the procurement of the *services* associated with the assets. The public sector client seeks to purchase the services provided by the asset, not the asset itself. This is an important perspective on capital projects. If they are seen less as physical assets and more as a stream of services to be made available over time, then ownership of the asset becomes a peripheral issue.

If an NHS trust needs the services of a new hospital, it does not need to own the building. This principle applies to the whole public sector. Whether the focus is on roads, prisons, education or whichever sector, what is needed by the public sector are the underlying services from the capital investment, not ownership of the physical assets associated with the investments. The ownership of the assets carries with it risks which have nothing to do with the particular service being delivered. The change of emphasis is also reflected in the new vocabulary which comes with PFI. The public sector now procures 'custodial services' instead of prisons, 'hospital or non-clinical services' instead of hospitals, 'highway services' instead of roads, 'facilities and property management services' instead of buildings, 'information technology services' instead of hardware and software equipment, and so on.

The effect of this shift (i.e. contracting for services rather than for assets) on public sector capital expenditure is important. PFI shifts lumpy, up-front capital expenditure into regular service payments (current expenditure) over a long-term contract period (typically 30 years). The contractual commitment by the public sector to purchase services from the private sector over several decades beyond the creation of the asset has important implications for controlling future public expenditure.

Notwithstanding this observation, it could be argued that the public expenditure implications of PFI, as opposed to conventional procurements, are more apparent than real. Under the latter, there is no long-term contract, but expenditure would still need to be committed to maintain the asset in working condition. This, of course, assumes that there is a continuing need for the asset. Unless there is some overarching central control to monitor the revenue consequences of PFI commitments across government departments, PFI does, indeed, pose considerable risk to controlling public expenditure. This concern is now being addressed (House of Commons Treasury Committee 1996, pp. xi–xii). Other differences and similarities between PFI and conventional procurements are described in the section below.

PFI versus traditional method of procurement

PFI represents a fundamental shift in the way in which services are delivered. It is instructive to compare and contrast how this approach differs from conventional public sector procurements (*see* Figure 1.1).

Under a conventional procurement, the public sector procurer would:

- design the specification for the asset in detail
- seek competitive tenders for the construction work (and subsequently for equipping it in the case of buildings)
- acquire the site and take responsibility for all preparatory work (e.g. obtaining planning permission)
- finance the project and begin payment for the asset from the beginning of the construction work
- manage the project
- provide all operational services directly or contract them out (usually to a number of different service providers)
- assume responsibility for maintaining the asset throughout its life (including acceptance of all or most of the risks associated with it).

Under PFI, the public sector would:

- specify the services it wishes to procure by producing an output specification
- seek competitive tenders for provision of the services (including the funding of the project)
- allocate project risks optimally between the service provider and procurer
- enter into a long-term contractual relationship for the provision of the services (including equipments and support services)
- link payments to the availability of the facility and the contractor's performance (and abate or discontinue payments when the agreed standards have been breached)
- have no interest in the ownership and management of the facility (hence no liability for residual value risks on the expiry of the contract).

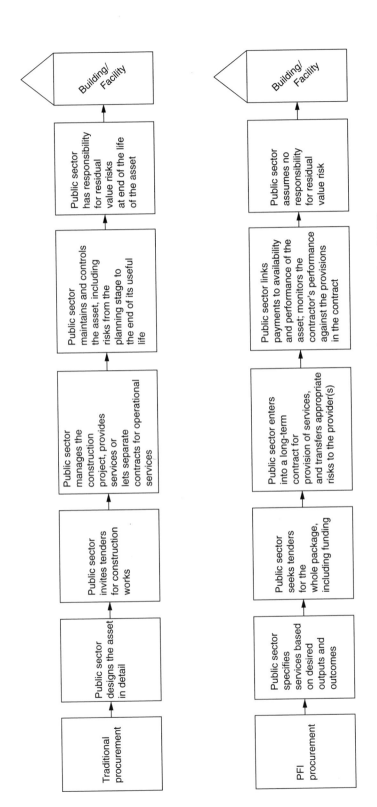

Figure 1.1: PFI compared to traditional procurement (adapted from Audit Commission 1998).

Models of PFI

Services sold to the public sector

At the launch of PFI, three types of projects were identified: (i) projects which are designed, built, financed and operated by the private sector and where the costs are recouped by selling the services provided from the facility mainly or entirely to the public sector (e.g. hospitals and prisons); (ii) where the capital cost of the project is split between the public and private sectors with overall responsibility resting with the private sector (e.g. a road designed to reduce congestion where the social benefit is believed to outweigh the revenue the project could generate); and (iii) financially free standing projects where the costs of the project are funded entirely by private money and recovered by means of direct charges to the end user (e.g. a road funded by direct tolls on the user).

The first model (services sold exclusively or mainly to the public sector) may be described as the 'classical model' as it is by far the most prevalent type of PFI transaction. Under this partnership arrangement, the private sector takes responsibility for designing, building, financing and operating the facility based on a clearly defined, but not prescriptive, output-based specification.

Typically, the private sector establishes a special purpose vehicle (SPV) across a wide range of sectors, including construction companies, facilities management providers, information technology providers, equipment providers, maintenance providers, specialist manufacturers and other providers with a proven track record in delivering the type of services specified in the output-based specification. A fundamental goal of the private sector is to create synergies across the design, build, finance and operation phases. Other private sector players include equity providers (i.e. those providing equity but not providing a service to the SPV) and financiers (primarily banks which normally provide long-term senior debt or, in the case of capital markets funding, lead managers/underwriters and a monoline credit insurer providing credit enhancement for the bonds sold to investors). Further details on the composition of a typical consortium and the nature of the contractual relationships are provided in Morrison and Owen (1996).

A contract is awarded by the public sector to the private sector, typically for 30 years. The contract transfers risks from the public sector to the private sector, based on the principle of 'optimal risk allocation'. This means allocating risk to the party who is best placed to manage it.

Payments are not made until the facility and associated services have been accepted as fit for purpose by the procuring entity. The client should make a single unitary payment each period (usually monthly or quarterly in arrears), rather than separating the payment stream into those for the financing of the underlying asset and those for the provision of support services. The conditions and standards to be met by the operator must be clearly set out in the contract. The payment mechanism should be designed to ensure that the operator is exposed to the normal commercial risk and rewards of ownership of assets. Ideally, the whole payment stream should be *variable*. This may be divided between volume and availability risks. If the standards set out in the Service Level Agreement are breached, cumulative penalty points are scored which will result in deductions in payments. Poor performance, depending on its severity and duration, may ultimately constitute a 'termination event'.

If the deal is properly structured and sufficient risk transfer is achieved, the transaction will satisfy the requirements of what accountants call an 'operating lease'. That is to say, it will be regarded as a purchase of access to and use of serviced assets by the public sector, and will, consequently, be capitalised on the private sector's balance sheet. Under these circumstances, PFI will have a beneficial impact on the public sector's borrowing requirement.

Note, although related to privatisation and contracting out, PFI is different from both of these policies. For example, unlike privatisation, the public sector continues to retain a role as the main purchaser of the service and enabler of its provision. Unlike contracting out, the private sector is a provider of both the capital asset and the services.

Joint ventures and financially free-standing projects

Under joint ventures, the costs of the project are subsidised from public funds rather than being recovered entirely through charges on the end users. The subsidy can take various forms, although the public sector's role is usually limited to a contribution towards asset development. Operational control resides with the private sector. Typical examples of this type of project include the Docklands Light Railway Extension, Manchester's Metrolink and Business Park developments.

Financially free-standing projects are also design, build, finance and operate (DBFO) schemes which are wholly funded by the private sector. The private sector recovers its costs entirely from charges for services to the final users. Examples of this type of project are toll roads and bridges (the Dartford River Crossing and the Second Severn Bridge), and the Royal Armouries.

The government can be a customer, but payments for any services which it purchases should be made on a full commercial basis. There should be no acceptance of risk on the part of the government from the point where the private sector assumes responsibility for the project. Government involvement in such projects is usually limited to enabling activities (e.g. assisting with planning permission, licensing and other statutory procedures).

Although these are the three dominant models of PFI which have been implemented to date, other models of PFI/PPP will undoubtedly emerge over time as the partnership between the public and private sectors becomes cemented. The government does not favour any particular model over other possible models of private sector participation. Indeed, it has made a conscious policy to encourage innovation and experimentation in recognition of the heterogeneous circumstances of the various organisations involved in such partnerships.

Note that PFI should not be misconstrued with privatisation simply because it involves the private sector. Privatisation involves removing certain services entirely from the public sector and giving complete control to the private sector. The private sector assumes all of the risk and is subject to regulation laid down by statute. PFI involves partnerships and risk-sharing with the private sector, with each party bringing to the project their comparative advantage, and managing the risks which they are best placed to manage.

Sources of PFI benefits

For any partnership between the public and private sectors to flourish, both parties must benefit from the relationship. PFI/PPP is founded on this principle. It has the potential to offer colossal benefits to both parties. For example, it opens up new business opportunities to the private sector, which, previously, have been the exclusive preserve of the public sector. The risk transfer involved in PFI transactions provides greater scope for higher profits if the private sector manages these risks well.

In principle, PFI can improve value for money to the public sector in the provision of services through:

- better allocation of risk, taking into account the respective abilities of the public and private sectors to manage the risks associated with the project
- better incentives to perform as payments are directly linked to the contractor's performance
- close integration of service needs with design and construction to promote maximum efficiency in the use of the assets over the long term
- ensuring that assets are fully fit for purpose but no more than is strictly necessary (i.e. removing the historical tendency to over-design or gold-plate)
- a clearer focus on the respective responsibilities of the public and private sectors which more clearly reflects the strengths of each. The public sector can concentrate on *what* service should be provided, leaving the private sector to consider *how* it can best be done
- a continuing commercial incentive for efficiency throughout the design, asset creation, maintenance and operation of the project. By adopting a whole-life approach to the procurement, building the asset and disappearing (with no regard to long-term operating costs of the building) becomes a thing of the past
- sweating the capital: more potential for efficiencies and for shared experience by the provision of assets supplying a wider range of customers (e.g. renting surplus building facilities or other services to 'third party' users, scope for companies to recover costs of facilities through user charges – restaurants, car parks, laundry, etc.)
- economies of scale from bigger schemes where capital assets are shared (e.g. clinical waste incinerators)
- designing the asset to enhance its resale value or its capacity to be transferred to alternative uses after the expiry of the contract
- PFI/PPP offers the prospect of more as well as better quality projects. If such deals provide genuine savings compared to the conventionally funded alternative, they will release resources for other projects. Joint venture projects also enable projects to proceed which the public sector could not have afforded on its own.

In addition, projects may go ahead under the PFI earlier than they would proceed under the conventional funded route since they involve a smoother flow of payments over the project life. For example, the cost of building the facility is spread over the life of the contract, rather than a lumpy capital outlay while the facility is being constructed which would have been the case under the traditional route. PFI also provides scope for the government to plan its expenditure better. Forward spending commitments become more transparent and certain. The cyclicality of the capital programme should improve as it is now replaced with a steady stream of service payments.

There are also potential macroeconomic benefits arising from the greater innovation and continuous improvement emphasised in PFI transactions and, to a lesser extent, more efficient working relationship and closer integration between the different sectors and business units involved in such transactions. More investment in public infrastructure and improved public services should raise the productive capacity of the economy and result in improved competitiveness.

PFI also heightens the public sector's awareness of risks and the need to manage it cost-effectively. Up till the 1990s, public sector projects were proverbial for the poor management of risks, particularly those which arise during the construction phase of a project. Some spectacular examples include: (i) the Thames Barrier (initially costed at £350m, but outturn construction cost was over £1 billion), (ii) the Limehouse Link road (costed at £142m, but final cost was £293m), and Trident Submarine and Berth (costed at £100m, but final cost was £314m) (cited in House of Commons Treasury Committee 1996). Although funded differently, the Channel Tunnel example is also instructive of how costs can escalate when risks are not comprehensively identified and assessed. The scheme was estimated at £2.5 billion in 1985 prices but delays added to the overall cost which resulted in more than double the original estimate (Oxford Economic Research Associates Ltd 1996).

The reasons for the public sector's poor record in delivering projects within the planned budget and timescale are complex. However, among the reasons often cited are poor management, the tendency to make frequent changes to the specification for the particular asset and the tendency to budget for the best possible outcome rather than the most likely (i.e. the problem of 'appraisal optimism'). Moreover, even if the public sector were to deliver capital projects within the planned budgets, it has been suggested that these projects could be delivered more cost-effectively by the private sector since the public sector has a tendency to follow higher technical standards or to over-engineer the asset (i.e. the problem of 'gold-plating'). The private sector, on the other hand, has an incentive to strike a balance between cost, financial return and risk.

Commentators on the policy frequently note that these benefits are largely a matter of faith rather than being grounded in any firm evidence. As Glaister puts it, '[it is based on] a belief that if you put something in service procurement to the private sector that was previously in the public sector, there is an economic law that says you will save about 20 per cent' (cited in House of Commons Treasury Committee 1996, p. 48). This appears to be borne out by the experience of the Northern Line and London Bus tendering procurements. Glaister argues that these efficiencies were largely achieved from greater flexibility in the use of labour and the terms on which they are employed compared to what is generally possible under the public sector. He also alludes to the incentives offered under PFI to improve the design of assets in order to reduce maintenance and operating costs. This benefit would be difficult to secure from conventional public sector procurement.

Evidence from other procurements under PFI-type arrangements claim savings up to 25%. The 'Competing for Quality' programme estimates savings of 25% on Whitehall activities. The Bridgend and Fazerley prisons projects claim average benefits in excess of 10% over the public sector alternative. Blakenhurst Prison – now under private management – is achieving 14% savings over the public sector alternative (Confederation of British Industry 1996, p. 13). The CBI further notes 'Strategic outsourcing by the private sector, often including capital elements within the deal, has typically achieved savings of around 30%' (p. 13).

The argument of those who question the PFI's ability to satisfy the value-for-money test is generally based on the relative cost of capital available to the public and private sector. It is asserted that the government can borrow more cheaply than the private sector. Glaister (1996) argues that private sector capital may be as high as 6–9 percentage points above the gilt rate.

Although superficially attractive, there is no firm evidence to support this claim. There is counter evidence to suggest that this argument is only true if the risks associated with individual projects are excluded from the discussion. Klein contends: 'If taxpayers were remunerated for the risk they assume in the case of tax-financed projects, then *ex ante* there would be no capital cost advantage to government finance. The risk premium on government finance would, in principle, be no different from that of private investors. There is thus no justification on the basis of capital cost advantage for government funding or guaranteeing the provision of private goods or services' (Klein 1997, p. 29). Large companies also have some of the same advantages as government. Just as government can distribute the risks associated with a project among a large number of people, large corporations can also distribute risks among a large number of shareholders. They should, therefore, be able to obtain finance at broadly similar rates as government, particularly if the risks faced by the project are familiar (*see* Chapter 4 for further details).

It could be argued that the risks surrounding PFI projects are still not familiar to financiers, hence, on balance, there is a risk premium on private sector capital compared to the cost of government finance. However, this is not sufficient to render PFI inferior on value-for-money grounds. The argument is something of a red herring because it is still possible, in principle, for higher financing costs to be outweighed by efficiencies from other aspects of the PFI package, particularly the design, build and operate elements. Ultimately, this debate can only be resolved by empirical evidence. The evidence reported in this book goes some way to illuminate this controversy, particularly evidence from the two case studies discussed in Chapters 7 and 8.

Policy background: old wine in new bottles?

The government has, for some considerable time, been promoting the involvement of the private sector in the provision of public infrastructure and services. The first major schemes originated from the so-called 'Ryrie rules', named after Sir William Ryrie, chairman of the committee set up by the National Economic Development Council in 1981 to review the investment rules for nationalised industries and to devise criteria under which private finance might be introduced into public sector schemes.

The two main rules were: (i) privately funded projects should be tested against publicly funded alternatives and demonstrate better value for money, and (ii) as a general rule, such projects (i.e. privately funded) should not be additional to public expenditure provision. They should be matched by equivalent cuts in public capital.

These rules made it almost impossible for private sector capital to be harnessed to fund public sector projects. The private sector was vociferous in its criticisms of these obsolete rules. In a wide-ranging report, the construction arm of the National Economic Development Organisation called attention to the constraints which these rules were imposing on the private sector (*see* Box 1.1). The government was swift to respond. In a speech in 1989, John Major remarked 'the view often prevails that "the Treasury" or "the Ryrie rules" are a huge stumbling block to greater private sector participation in the provision of infrastructure. The Ryrie rules are thought to be incomprehensible, and to hamper private finance by setting impossible hurdles' (cited in Heald 1996, p. 577).

The rules were relaxed in 1989 so that private funding would no longer have to be substitutional. The universal requirement to develop

---

Box 1.1: Some constraints on private investment in infrastructure

- Long and costly consultation and planning procedures
- Traditional perceptions of public services limit extent to which costs can be recouped through charges
- Land assembly sometimes possible only through compulsory purchase
- Lack of formal channels for private sector to identify and define projects needed by government
- Lack of assurance that projects will be protected from competition by subsequent government decisions
- Heavy front-end costs and difficulty of sharing or spreading risks

Source: cited in Terry (1996, p. 11)

---

public sector comparators (PSCs) to benchmark private sector proposals for value for money was also scrapped. PSCs were not required in cases where a project involves no public money or for projects which would not have gone ahead other than as a PFI project. In such cases, competition was seen as the mechanism for ensuring value for money (Private Finance Panel, November 1995, pp. 19–20).

Norman Lamont dealt the last blow to the Ryrie rules in 1992 on the occasion of his Autumn Statement when he announced 'important changes' in the rules applying to private finance by public sector bodies. It was hoped that the more permissive framework provided by PFI would create the right incentives for the public and private sectors to develop mutually beneficial partnerships. As Stephen Dorrell, former Health Secretary, observes, PFI was designed to correct a situation where 'the public sector was missing both extra access to capital and extra access to good management that could come through a proper partnership with the private sector' (cited in House of Commons Treasury Committee 1996, p. viii).

It was made clear that an effective working relationship between public and private sectors must be predicated on:

- a genuine transfer of risk to the private sector based on the principle of optimal allocation
- projects which yield value for money
- selecting private sector partners through open competition.

However, developments in the policy from 1992–97 reveal that what was required to make the partnership work in practice was poorly understood at the time. The result was mounting criticism of the policy during this period and slow take-up in key sectors, including the NHS sector. The vast majority of these criticisms were commercially motivated.

Many of these criticisms are summarised in the Commons Treasury Committee report (1996) and the CBI's report (1996). They include:

- lack of a strategic approach to the planning of projects
- lack of guidance and skills (especially in public sector bodies)
- compulsory, indiscriminate testing of all projects for private finance
- excessive transaction costs arising from a protracted procurement process
- inappropriate risk allocation
- a lack of assurance and legislative guarantee that contracts would be honoured (a major problem in the health and local authority sectors).

In a similar vein, the Labour Party's manifesto in 1996 called attention to the problems which dogged the policy:

> A Labour administration will overcome the problems that have plagued the PFI at a national level. We will set priorities between projects, saving time and expense: we will seek a realistic allocation of risk between the partners to a project; and will ensure that best practice is spread throughout Government . . . Labour will . . . end the delays, sort out the confusion and develop new forms of public/ private partnership that work better and protect the interests of the NHS. Labour is opposed to the privatisation of clinical services.

The Bates review, which was swiftly commissioned by the new Labour administration in May 1997 to reinvigorate the PFI, addressed a number of these issues. The review was carried out against the background of Labour's 12-point plan for successful partnership with the private sector (*see* Box 1.2). Its wide-ranging recommendations were accepted in full by the Government and included:

- stronger central direction and fundamental changes in the institutional structure (e.g. by replacing the Private Finance Panel and its Executive with a new Treasury Taskforce with wide-ranging powers to sign off the commercial viability of all significant projects before the procurement process begins)
- strengthening of departmental private finance units (PFUs)
- development of expertise within the public sector (e.g. production of guidance manuals, providing training to civil servants, and

Box 1.2: Labour's 12-point plan for public/private partnerships

1 PFI deals already signed, or accepted as operationally and financially viable, will proceed without delay

2 Every potential partnership will be subject to a more rigorous appraisal early in its life, so contractors, funders and operators do not squander time and resources on projects which are unlikely to work and the public sector avoids 'wish list' schemes

3 We will draw up guidance on tendering for partnership projects, in consultation with the National Audit Office, the Audit Commission and the Accounts Commission for Scotland

4 Where possible, we will set a timetable for each project's tendering process to give potential private partners an indication of when a decision can be expected on a project

5 We will urgently review the existing legislative framework, issue guidance and, where appropriate, enact new legislation to ensure that public bodies have the necessary legal power to enter into contracts

6 We will ensure that the guidance on risk transfer and value for money, including templates, is kept up to date, in consultation with public and private sector interests

7 We will seek to develop a clear and consistent policy on generic risks – for example the approach to changes in government health and safety policy or the treatment of contaminated land

8 We will encourage a wide range of partnership deals, including public/private joint ventures

9 The Private Finance Panel will be strengthened and given a specific remit to streamline procedures, develop standard forms of contract and cut red tape

10 We will encourage the rapid dissemination of best practice throughout Whitehall and the regions

11 We will require government to involve small business in partnership deals where possible

12 We will maintain prudent control on public sector revenue commitments to partnership deals and public sector liabilities in joint ventures, following consultation with the relevant public bodies

Source: Labour Party business manifesto (1996)

establishing a dedicated library in the Treasury with PFI material and good practice templates)
* prioritisation of projects
* end to universal testing of projects for private finance
* grouping small projects together to make them more attractive to the private sector and to improve value for money to the public sector
* simplification of the approval process
* the enactment of legislations to empower public sector bodies to enter into PFI contracts
* standardisation of the process (e.g. contracts) to reduce time and transaction costs.

These reforms have already begun to bear fruit. Box 1.3 provides an indication of the extent to which PFI has penetrated the various public sector departments. Other 'significant projects' have since been added to the list.

Box 1.3: The Taskforce's significant projects

Cabinet Office
GCHQ – new accommodation project

Customs and Excise
Assistance with proposals for provision of office accommodation
IS/IT infrastructure

Ministry of Defence
Colchester Garrison
Development of MoD – wide water and sewerage proposals
Heavy equipment transportation
MoD main building refurbishment
White fleets (non-deployable vehicles such as cars, coaches, etc.)

Department for Education and Employment
Dudley MBC, schools IT network (local authority)
Employment Service IT partnership project
Stoke on Trent, schools estate (local authority)

Department of Environment, Transport and the Regions
A13 Thames Gateway DBFO
Assistance with proposals for wider PPPs for London Underground
Channel Tunnel rail link
Connect (London Underground)

Development of MOT computerisation proposals (Vehicle Inspectorate)
Hereford and Worcester, waste management (local authority)
New Scottish Air Traffic Control Centre (CAA)
Power (London Underground)
Prestige (London Transport)

Foreign and Commonwealth Office
Global telecoms project

Northern Ireland Office
Development of PPPs in the water industry, including Bangor and Kinnegar Sewerage Projects (DoE)

Department of Health
Bishop Auckland Hospitals NHS Trust
Bromley Hospitals NHS Trust
Calderdale Healthcare NHS Trust
Carlisle Healthcare NHS Trust
Greenwich Healthcare NHS Trust
Hereford Hospitals NHS Trust
North Durham Acute NHS Trust
South Manchester University Hospitals NHS Trust
South Tees Acute Hospital NHS Trust
Swindon and Marlborough NHS Trust
Wellhouse NHS Trust
Worcester Royal Infirmary NHS Trust

Home Office
Central London Estate
Marchington and Onley Prisons
IT2000
Public safety radio communication project
QUANTUM (IT infrastructure for prisons)

Inland Revenue
Assistance with proposals for provision of office accommodation

Lord Chancellor's Department
Hereford and Worcester, Magistrates' Court (local authority)
LIBRA Magistrates' Court IT Services

National Savings
Development of PPPs

Scottish Office
Development of Glasgow District
Heating system proposals (Glasgow City Council)
Development of Glasgow Secondary School Estate proposals (Glasgow City Council)
Falkirk Schools (Falkirk Council)
Hairmyres and Stonehouse Hospitals NHS Trust
Law Hospital NHS Trust
Royal Infirmary of Edinburgh NHS Trust

Department of Social Security
ACCORD (IT infrastructure project)
Assistance with ADAPT (Benefits Agency field offices)

Department of Trade and Industry
ELGAR (electronic government through administrative re-engineering)
Welsh Office
A55
Baglan Hospital

Local Government PFI projects

Department of the Environment, Transport and the Regions
Local Authority Scheme

1997/1998
Isle of Wight, waste management – signed
LB Brent, street lighting
LB Harrow, office IT – signed
LB Islington, depot and vehicle services
LB Lambeth, depot and vehicle services – signed
Manchester CC, housing energy services
Kirklees, waste management
Hereford and Worcester, waste management
Kent CC, strategic IT
North East Derbyshire, social housing

1998/1999
LB Tower Hamlets, housing energy services
Bournemouth BC, library
LB Hackney, technology learning centre
Norfolk CC, salt storage facilities
North Wiltshire, property rationalisation

Department for Education and Employment

1997/1998
Dorset CC, Colfox School – signed
Kingston upon Hull, primary school
LB Lewisham, schools catering facilities

1998/1999
Birmingham City Council, 10 schools package
Dudley MBC, schools IT network
LB Enfield, secondary school
Manchester City Council, Temple primary school
Westminster City Council, Pimlico school
Staffordshire CC, two schools
Portsmouth City Council – secondary school

1998/1999 or 1999/2000
Stoke on Trent, schools estate

Department of Health

1997/1998
LB Harrow, care facilities
LB Westminster, residential home
Surrey CC, residential homes

1998/1999
Dudley MBC, multi-use facility
LB Richmond, residential homes

Home Office

1997/1998
Derbyshire, Police Divisional HQ
Derbyshire, Ilkeston Police Station
Northumbria, police mounted facility
Wiltshire, police air support

1998/1999
Greater Manchester, fire station/HQ
Abingdon Area HQ, traffic base and sector station
Norfolk Constabulary Operations and Coms Service

Lord Chancellor's Department

1998/1999
Hereford and Worcester, Magistrates' Court

1998/1999 or 1999/2000
Derbyshire, Magistrates Court
Humberside, Magistrates Court
Manchester, Magistrates Court

Source: Davidson 1998

Concluding remarks

This chapter has demonstrated that the attempt to involve the private sector in the delivery of public services has a long history. The PFI is the latest attempt to remove whatever obstacles remain after the Ryrie rules have been reformed. On this reading, PFI may be viewed as 'old wine in new bottles'.

Despite its slow progress prior to 1997, the way is now clear for harnessing the benefits from public–private partnerships. This new approach to procuring public services has now taken root in all public sector organisations, including the NHS and local authorities, where it proved particularly difficult to get the policy airborne. Although the organisations occupy different positions on the PFI learning curve, it will not be long before the laggards catch up with the more experienced sectors. Books like this which document case study evidence have a major role to play in transferring many of the costly and painful lessons learned to date.

CHAPTER TWO

PFI in health: strategic planning and prioritisation of projects

Since the launch of PFI in 1992, the NHS has been actively seeking to exploit the benefits of collaboration with the private sector to develop and modernise the capital infrastructure needed to support the delivery of patient care. NHS Trusts, PCGs, health authorities and other project sponsors are required to rigorously explore private finance options where appropriate, and where this could lead to improved value for money. This chapter explains the nature of the PFI product in the health sector, progress to date, the capital procurement process in the NHS and the way projects are prioritised for PFI testing.

The chapter also discusses the importance of proper planning before commencement of the procurement. It calls attention to the importance of the output-based specification, payment mechanism, risk allocation, contract terms and a number of other important prerequisites for the procurement.

Role of capital in delivering health services

The NHS estate occupies some 16 500 hectares of land and comprises some 1400 hospitals, clinics, ambulance stations and other capital infrastructure. The capital value of this estate amounts to an estimated £24 billion. The capital spend for 1997/98 on constructing, equipping, improving and modernising the capital stock was £1.6 billion.

Maintenance costs per year amount to some £390m, and energy consumption accounts for a further £216m (NHSE 1997).

Capital is a major factor of production in producing healthcare. As providers of health services, NHS trusts invest capital to:

- maintain the quantity and quality of current services (e.g. by replacing obsolete equipment)
- enable existing services to expand
- enable new services to be provided (e.g. from rationalisation of facilities)
- provide patients with better access to healthcare services
- improve quality of services (e.g. to keep pace with statutory requirements – fire, safety, hygiene standards, etc.; patient expectations, professional standards and medical advance)
- optimise the use of the current asset base and bring about greater efficiency in the utilisation of staff and other resources
- enable rationalisation and coherence in service delivery (thus making for more cost-effective and sustainable service provision)
- release savings for reinvestment
- address staffing issues (recruitment and retention problems) and meet the requirements of medical education, training and research
- facilitate other strategic changes (e.g. new models for delivering services, national priorities and policy imperatives, such as the shift to a primary-care led NHS, closure of long stay institutions, etc.).

Boxes 2.1 and 2.2 provide examples of how capital is being used to support delivery of government objectives for the NHS. Both schemes are based on different models of care. The Central Middlesex Hospital (CMH) project is essentially a hospital without beds, while the Norfolk and Norwich scheme is a more efficient variant of the existing model of care.

The PFI health product

PFI in the NHS differs fundamentally from the way the initiative has developed in most other areas of government. This is largely a consequence of the sensitivities surrounding delivery of *core* clinical services.

Unlike the prisons sector, for example, where the *whole* service is typically delivered by the private sector, NHS projects undertaken

Box 2.1: Example of using capital as a catalyst for change – the ACAD Centre (Central Middlesex Hospital)

This is an innovative model of care, which originated in the push to increase the use of day-care procedures in the NHS and the consequent reduction in in-patient beds.

Faced with a hotch-potch of poorly interfaced departments in low quality building stock – some stretching back to the 19th century, huge backlog maintenance costs and a shortage of capital investments, CMH chose to use capital investment not just to renew a major element of their capital stock but to re-invent the purpose for which the hospital will be used.

The resulting Ambulatory Care and Diagnostic Centre (ACAD) is effectively a hospital without beds with the objectives of:

- separating secondary-level elective day-care from emergency care
- providing improved quality elective care at significantly lower costs
- combining surgical, medical and imaging facilities within new, purpose-designed accommodation
- reorganising of clinical care protocols and staffing arrangements to maximise the range of out-patient care
- creating added-value through involving the private sector in providing interventionary and diagnostic imaging equipment, electronic patient records and scheduling systems, and integrated facilities management.

The design concept for the ACAD was informed by innovative polyclinics and ambulatory care centres in the United States. It included high-tech imaging intervention space, a patient zone, a series of green courts, a public zone connecting the two and a 'town edge' comprising offices, a restaurant and various other facilities.

The importance which the Trust attached to good design reflected its remarkable awareness of the link between the built environment and patient outcomes. For example, research has linked poor design to anxiety, delirium, elevated blood pressure, increased need for pain medication and longer hospital stays following surgery.

Source: cited in Royal Fine Art Commission (1997)

Box 2.2: The Norfolk and Norwich PFI scheme

The Norfolk and Norwich PFI hospital project is the biggest in the history of the NHS. With a capital cost of £214m, the new hospital will replace the Trust's two existing acute hospitals. The new hospital, comprising 900 000 square feet of accommodation and 809 beds, will be built in a 63-acre greenfield site owned by the Trust over four years under a consortium led by John Laing Construction.

The anticipated benefits include:

- economies from single-site working
- better access to patients, especially those who require a range of treatments and who will now receive them from one site
- space for development and improvement of services in line with medical advances
- reduced maintenance costs
- enhanced opportunities to strengthen research and development links with the University of East Anglia and the Norwich Research Park
- local economies (e.g. employment opportunities) resulting from a major construction project.

The then Health Minister, Alan Milburn, speaking on the day the deal reached financial close said: 'I am delighted that construction will now start on the largest contract in the largest new hospital programme in the history of the NHS. **They will now get the brand new hospital for the 21st century that they deserve – the best modern healthcare available. Today's announcement is part of the Government's wider commitment to modernise the NHS and provide newer and better services for the public. An NHS fit for the new century'** (*PFI Journal* 3(1): 46; emphasis added).

under the PFI will generally be limited to the design, construction, finance and operation of building and support services. In the over-whelming majority of cases, the NHS organisation continues to be the employer of clinical staff. Private sector responsibility is not extended into the clinical area. Note, the main component of a hospital's operating costs is clinical labour, typically accounting for some 70% of the cost base.

Subject to this constraint, the private sector is expected to deliver a wide range of facilities for the NHS. Box 2.3 indicates the types of opportunities which are open to the private sector in the health sector.

The delivery of many of these services by private sector operators is not novel. As noted in the previous chapter, competitive tendering for such services has been around since the early 1980s. What is new is the way these services are packaged, the approach to the procurement, the form and duration of the contract, and the emphasis on risk transfer and value for money.

Some commentators have argued that the peculiarities of the health product rules out the ability of the private sector to make any significant impact on improving value for money in this sector. For example, Manning (1996) argues '. . . the PFI process, as it stands, not only results in a tendency for projects to be unaffordable but crucially fails to deliver the best solution for the NHS and the taxpayer, both in terms of costs and the strategic development of the NHS as a whole' (p. 5). For Manning, the fundamental cause of this poor performance stems from the nature of the healthcare PFI product and the private sector's inability to have a major impact on the bulk of the operating costs of a hospital (i.e. the cost of clinical services). Unlike infrastructure projects in the transport sector, a clever or innovative design for the building, a shorter building period, reduced capital costs for the facility and other efficiencies introduced by the private sector will, consequently, only produce a small impact on the total operating costs of a hospital.

Manning's observations suggest the more services – both non-clinical and clinical – are included in PFI contracts the greater the potential to increase value for money to the public sector. The model he advocates is similar to the one adopted in the prison's sector where the whole of the prison operations, including employment of prison managers, falls within the responsibility of the private sector. There is evidence to suggest the procurement of the first two prisons deals – Bridgend and Fazakerley – produced substantial savings. Both prisons came into operation ahead of schedule, twice as quickly as prisons following the conventional route. The Prison Service estimated that the Bridgend contract produced savings of £53m at 1995 prices compared with the public sector alternative. This has been independently corroborated by the NAO who, in fact, identified a number of ways in which this value-for-money gap could have been further widened (NAO 1998, p. v).

The issue raised by Manning and others is about scale of benefits, rather than whether PFI passes the value-for-money test in the health sector. The value-for-money test in the health sector is rigorous. Unlike some other departments, there is a requirement for project sponsors to develop a fit-for-purpose PSC and to fully comply with all three value-for-money tests discussed in Chapter 5. It is not sufficient to rely on competition to choose the economically most advantageous PFI bid. Independent work undertaken by KPMG and The Major Contractors

Group (1998) found evidence of significant net savings from the early health schemes. As schemes in this sector mature and the partnership with the private sector solidifies, the savings will become more pronounced.

Box 2.3: Services which are currently within the scope of PFI/PPP agreements

Information management and technology
Accommodation
Property and building maintenance
Residential accommodation
Grounds and gardens maintenance
Equipment maintenance
Domestic services
Catering
Laundry
Waste disposal
Pest control
Portering
Security
Non-emergency patient transport
Courier services
Financial services
Car parking
Telecommunications
Energy and utilities
Sterile supply services
Stores
Reception
Postal services

Progress to date

Since the launch of PFI in 1992, trusts and health authorities are required to consider PFI to meet their capital needs where appropriate. Guidance has been developed to support compliance with the policy, the most recent being *The PFI Manual* (NHSE 1999) which replaced

HSG 95(15) (NHSE 1995). In June 1994, a database was created to match potential private sector providers to NHS projects by the firm New-church and Company.

By July 1995, 324 private sector companies and 400 NHS organisations were registered on the database. Reportedly, 133 projects were either completed or close to completion and a further 800 had been identified as suitable candidates for PFI, amounting to an estimated £2 billion in capital costs (Nash and Manning 1995). It is now common knowledge that the vast majority of the projects which were approved prior to May 1997 never got off the ground. Dartford and Gravesham, with a capital value of £115m, became the first PFI contract to be signed. This was only achieved in July 1997. The policy continues to prove difficult to apply in primary care, mental health and community care.

The reasons for the slow and disappointing take-up of the policy in the NHS are well known. They were, to a considerable degree, similar to those encountered by other public sector bodies, and which were tackled in the Bates review. Among the most significant problems in the health sector were the following.

Financiers' fears

Financiers expressed concerns about a number of risks, many of which stemmed from the NHS 'internal market', most notably risks such as:

- dissolution or bankruptcy of an NHS trust
- changes in purchasing strategy thus rendering a trust unviable (e.g. Suffolk Health Authority and East Norfolk Health Authority's decision to cease purchasing services from Anglian Harbours NHS Trust with effect from 31 August 1997 on account of poor trust performance)
- competition from other trusts – especially in inner cities like London where there are numerous providers
- perceived weaknesses of the management team in some trusts and high turnover of key personnel – including medical personnel
- the decentralised nature of trusts and perceived lack of clarity about what recourse can be made to the Secretary of State for Health in the event of a trust's default on their liabilities
- legality of an NHS trust's power to enter into PFI contracts (i.e. the so-called 'vires issue'). Financiers argued that the 1990 Act which established NHS trusts predates the introduction of PFI. Their fear was based on losses incurred in the past on local authorities'

contracts, including the decisions of the Court of Appeal in Credit Suisse vs Allerdale Borough Council. This contract was ruled to be ultra vires. The Consortia Credit Suisse lost £5m (*The Guardian*, April 1997). Similar losses were reported elsewhere for the same reason (e.g. private sector bodies that had contracts with Hammersmith and Fulham council).

Affordability

Put simply, affordability may be defined as the ability of health authorities and other commissioners of a trust's services to absorb the price implications of a PFI scheme. A scheme which is cost-effective to the public sector as a whole, based on the results of the economic appraisal, may not necessarily be affordable since the affordability test includes a number of costs which are not usually included in an economic appraisal. These include non-resource costs such as VAT, other forms of taxation, capital charges and intra-NHS costs. Moreover, the profiling of payments to the consortia and financiers may create mismatches between the client's income and expenditure in particular years.

A number of PFI projects, while supported by the economic appraisal, were delayed on account of affordability problems stemming from causes such as:

- weaknesses in the business case, for example ill-founded costing or revenue assumptions
- failure to factor in risk in the economic appraisal, especially at the crucial Outline Business Case (OBC) stage
- insufficient involvement of purchasers in the development of schemes which tended to grow in size and cost with no compensating health gain
- problems with the PFI process itself (for example, limited innovation in schemes, high transaction costs and other cost pressures)
- the short payback period demanded by financiers and the service providers. They insisted on recouping the cost of their capital over the period of the primary contract. The maturities for project finance was typically for 20 to 23 years whereas conventionally financed schemes would normally be amortised over the life of the asset (typically 60 years) under conventional finance. Purchasers therefore face higher prices under PFI during the early years of a PFI contract and lower prices towards the latter years.

Failure to prioritise schemes

Schemes were allowed to proceed with very little attention given to whether they were justified on health service grounds. The policy prior to May 1997 was derisively dubbed the policy of allowing 'a thousand weeds to bloom'. Although a plethora of schemes were 'approved' and a vast amount of resources were expended by both the NHS and private sector in the procurement process, not a single major hospital scheme had reached commercial and financial close prior to this date.

In response to the log jam, the new Labour administration announced a review of PFI in the NHS in June 1997. The review had three objectives: (i) to secure the PFI market, (ii) to improve the PFI process and (iii) to develop and improve the PFI product. The review has now been completed. The key recommendations appeared in the *Health Service Journal* (Dix 1999).

The review identified over 20 improvements to the PFI process (*see* Box 2.4). It also contained measures to promote PFI in the non-acute sectors. These include batching of smaller schemes as has happened in the education sector and developing pilot schemes. The vast majority of the problems which had previously impeded the PFI in the NHS have now been surmounted. The fears expressed by financiers and their lawyers about the vires of NHS trusts to engage in PFI contracts and the risks arising from possible bankruptcy or default on payments have been resolved by the swift enactment of the Residual Liabilities Act in May 1996 and the 1997 Vires Act. The NHS (Residual Liabilities) Act provides statutory power to the Secretary of State to dissolve an NHS trust if considered appropriate. Under such circumstances, the trust's liabilities will be transferred to another NHS organisation or the Secretary of State.

Affordability problems have been addressed by measures such as the introduction of risk-adjusted Outline Business Cases, greater involvement of commissioners in the development of schemes, 'smoothing funds' provided by the NHS Executive to help commissioners fund soundly conceived schemes during the early years of the contract when costs are relatively high, and greater central direction from the NHS Executive Headquarters and its Regional Offices (*see* Meara (1997) for further details). The policy of allowing a 'thousand flowers to bloom' has been replaced with a system based on rational planning and prioritisation, driven by an assessment of health service need, affordability, PFI ability, deliverability and market capacity (discussed below).

The new approach to PFI has begun to bear fruits. Considerable

Box 2.4: Proposed improvements to PFI procurement in the NHS

- A halving of trusts' PFI procurement costs (from 3 or 4 to 2 per cent of capital cost) and the time from when a project is first advertised to financial close (from an average of three years to 18 months)
- Withdrawal of government approval for schemes that are 'ailing' and fail to meet an agreed timetable. 'Stopped' schemes can be reconsidered in the next round of PFI projects only if problems are resolved
- Trusts with schemes over £25m must put up to six consortia through an extra pre-qualification stage. Once three have been shortlisted, two must be selected to work schemes up to an advanced stage before a preferred bidder is chosen
- Trusts with schemes over £25m should set out their business and services strategy in a strategic outline case for prioritisation by the NHS capital prioritisation advisory group
- Proposals should stem from the local strategy (to be embodied in the Health Improvement Programme) which health authorities (HAs) and primary care groups (PCGs) will have helped to formulate
- The main commissioner should be 'directly represented' on the project board for major schemes. Others may be involved 'as appropriate': 'It may be that both the HA and the primary care group should have a place on the project board'
- Affordability calculations should include whole-life costs, not just capital costs
- Trusts must publish the public sector comparator, 'unless, exceptionally, it can be convincingly demonstrated . . . that there will be minimal competition'
- Output specifications should be 'as fully developed as possible' before the scheme is tendered, and 'where possible' all formal public consultation completed before involvement of the private sector, and before outline planning permission on the site is obtained
- Openness and consultation are paramount, including publication of all key PFI project documents as well as a summary of the final contract
- Good employment practices and management should be a factor in determining value for money in the trust's choice of PFI partner. Unions should interview all preferred bidders and their views help inform the trust's decision
- For the most part, human resources issues 'should be tackled not in the specific NHS, but in the much broader context of the government's fairness at work legislation and the revision of TUPE'

Source: Dix (1999, p. 10)

progress has now been made in securing the market and improving the PFI process and product. Since May 1997, three tranches of schemes have been prioritised. The first two waves accounted for 25 major PFI hospital developments with a capital cost of almost £2.2 billion. The government has hailed this the biggest hospital programme in the 50-year history of the NHS.

1998 was undoubtedly a bonanza year in the PFI health market. A number of the first tranche of 14 prioritised schemes reached financial close, leaving four to reach this milestone. The remaining four schemes and some of the second wave of prioritised schemes can be expected to reach financial close before the end of 1999. The third wave of schemes whose announcement is imminent further attests to evidence of a buoyant and mature market in this sector. At the same time, effort is being made to adapt the classical DBFO approach to meet the particular requirements of schemes in the primary care, mental health and community care sectors. These include batching of schemes, relocating or locating schemes where they can maximise the returns to the private sector and, at the same time, meet the NHS' service requirements, and creating imaginative partnerships between GPs, NHS organisations and the private sector.

The NHS capital investment and prioritisation process

Among the most significant of the reforms introduced under the 1990 NHS and Community Care Act was the introduction of what has become known as the 'internal market'. Although the market is now being dismantled and replaced by a model based on partnerships, the NHS remains a decentralised organisation. Working in partnership with each other, the broad demarcation of responsibilities between NHS trusts and commissioners which prevailed prior to the introduction of the new White Paper has remained largely intact.

Commissioners continue to take the lead in implementing national health policy, assessing local healthcare needs, developing a commissioning strategy to meet local needs, commissioning services for local needs and ensuring services are delivered to the required standards. Over time, they are expected to relinquish direct commissioning responsibilities to primary care groups (PCGs). NHS trusts, on the other hand, continue to serve as *providers*, delivering services in response to the service strategy articulated in three-year Health

Improvement Programmes (HImP). This includes assuming prime responsibility for developing and implementing a capital investment strategy to meet service needs.

As noted previously, since May 1997 there has been greater central co-ordination of capital schemes. The NHS Capital Prioritisation Advisory Group (CPAG) was set up in 1997 to evaluate and make recommendations to Ministers on the prioritisation of major schemes in the NHS. These are publicly and privately financed schemes with a capital cost over £25m.

Strategic Outline Case

Schemes are prioritised on the basis of health service need, based on the information contained in the Strategic Outline Case (SOC). The SOC is produced before the Outline Business Case (OBC) and is designed to provide sufficient information to enable CPAG to consider the national priority of a scheme. All schemes prioritised for development will subsequently require OBC and Full Business Case (FBC) approval.

The first round of prioritisation takes place at Regional Office level. Regional Offices are responsible for deciding, based on strategic fit and regional priorities, which schemes should prepare a SOC. Those schemes demonstrating the highest health service need within the region will then be forwarded to CPAG for national prioritisation.

In summary, the prioritisation process involves the following steps:

- Step one: Regional Offices invite bids from trusts and their commissioners in the form of a SOC. They then select and prioritise schemes for consideration by CPAG.
- Step two: Regional Offices submit the SOCs for their selected schemes to CPAG for scrutiny by the Technical Sub-Committee (TSC). The TSC is an advisory group which provides technical advice to CPAG.
- Step three: The TSC advises CPAG on the schemes submitted. CPAG, in turn, supplements this advice with information gained about the proposed schemes from site visits and presentations made by their sponsors.
- Step four: CPAG considers the schemes submitted and makes recommendations to the NHS Executive Board and, subsequently, to Ministers.

Schemes that are selected by CPAG are required to proceed to the OBC stage. Proposals for schemes with a capital value of less than £25m will not be considered by CPAG and are not required to produce a SOC. However, such schemes will still have to set the strategic context for a proposed scheme in line with the requirement of the *Capital Investment Manual* (NHSE 1997) and produce an OBC. The process is illustrated below in Figure 2.1.

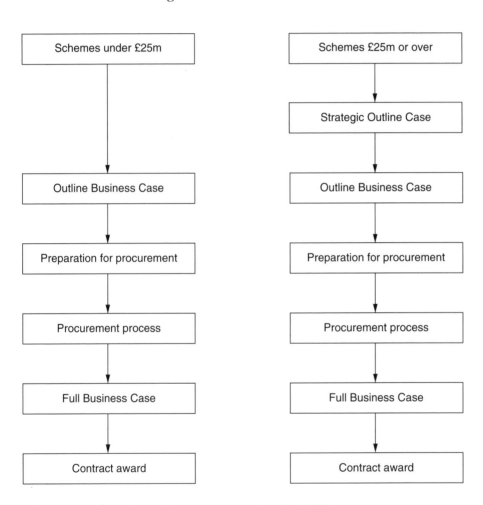

Figure 2.1: The private finance process in the NHS.

The Outline Business Case

Having made the case for change in the SOC, the aim of the OBC is to identify the preferred option which meets the strategic objectives. To avoid nugatory effort and inappropriate use of public funds, work on the OBC should not begin until the SOC has been approved.

The OBC should be supported by a rigorous investment appraisal. Chapter 5 discusses the steps involved in meeting this requirement. It should be developed in close collaboration with all stakeholders, particularly commissioners and the Regional Office.

The trust, Regional Office and the main commissioner and/or PCG should ensure that the preferred option identified in the OBC fully satisfies the strategic and health service objectives underlying the proposed scheme. The costs, benefits and risks associated with this option should be rigorously assessed over the life of the project. This option will normally be the one which meets the project objectives and delivers the greatest ratio of benefits to costs.

An option which provides the best value for money to the public sector will not necessarily be affordable to the trust and its commissioners. It is therefore important for the trust to undertake a financial appraisal to demonstrate the affordability of the preferred investment decision over its life span. Sensitivity analyses should be undertaken on the key assumptions underlying the cost of the preferred option.

Different scenarios should be modelled, including optimistic, neutral and pessimistic scenarios. The financial analysis should also make explicit allowance for the cost of risks, both those likely to be transferred to the private sector and those likely to be retained by the public sector. Support from the relevant commissioner(s) should be explicit and unequivocal (*see* Box 2.5).

The Full Business Case

The aim of the FBC is to identify the preferred method for funding the project and the preferred partner for meeting the trust's requirements. Approval should be sought from the NHS Executive before the scheme progresses to financial close.

Details of what to include in the FBC are discussed in Chapter 6. This chapter also discusses the timing for submission of the FBC and its inter-relationship with the procurement process.

Box 2.5: Conditions for commissioner support at OBC stage

On submission of the OBC, written evidence should be obtained from the main commissioners to show:

- they support the strategic objectives of the scheme proposed
- they are satisfied that the objectives of the business case are consistent with national initiatives and policy imperatives, as well as local priorities
- they support the model of care underlying the scheme
- they understand the practical and financial implications of the scheme
- they endorse the price and activity assumptions underlying the case
- they plan to purchase services at the levels and prices specified in the case (including over the duration of the contract)
- they can afford to pay for the services at the specified price
- all the appropriate public consultation processes have been completed
- the margins of leeway beyond which support must be revalidated have been agreed (usually +/−5%)

The requirement to consider PFI

It remains a challenge to identify which projects are suitable for PFI. The policy of universal testing for private finance has now been disbanded by the Paymaster General. If an NHS trust considers that a project has little chance of attracting private finance, and that the interests of the NHS would not be served by testing for PFI, it should put its case in writing to the relevant NHS Executive Regional Office. If the project is within the NHS trust's approval threshold, this decision should be made by board members and other local stakeholders. It should be remembered that even where a scheme is demonstrated to represent good value for money there can be no guarantee that public capital will be available to fund it. Opportunities should therefore be explored to find ways of making the scheme attractive for private finance. For example, small schemes could be packaged together.

The CBI has identified a useful set of characteristics for identifying *a*

Box 2.6: Favourable PFI project characteristics

- Output/service delivery driven (i.e. a properly specified output specification)
- Substantial operating content
- Significant scope for additional/alternative uses of the asset
- Scope for innovation in design
- Surplus assets intrinsic to the transaction
- Long contract term available
- Committed public sector management
- Political sensitivities manageable
- Risks primarily commercial in nature
- Substantial deals
- Complete or stand-alone operations to allow maximum synergies

Source: adapted from Exhibit 1 (CBI 1997, p. 16)

---

priori which schemes are suitable for PFI (*see* Box 2.6). This list may be further supplemented by the following (more pointed) set of test questions:

- Are there significant risks arising from the project which could be better managed by the private sector (e.g. construction and development risks)?
- Will the public sector gain extra flexibilities through a PFI solution?
- Will the private sector gain significant extra performance incentives over the life of the contract to produce a better outcome for both parties?
- Does the project offer additional scope to recover costs through income-generating activities or extra sales to third party markets (e.g. by enlarging the scheme to allow greater or additional use, adding extra facilities to meet the requirements of other users)?
- Is there scope for the private sector to reduce the capital costs, running costs or both sets of costs which arise from the scheme (e.g. by exploiting opportunities for economies of scale, more innovative design, using better technology)?
- Can the private sector make the facility easier to lease and re-let (e.g. by sizing it appropriately, changing the quality or the embodied technology to make it more attractive to secondary users)?

Pre-requisites for the procurement

One of the key recommendations of the Bates review is the need for proper preparation *before* the procurement begins. To state the obvious (which is often overlooked), a carefully planned procurement exercise is more likely to yield a good, value-for-money deal.

The Bates report and subsequent guidance issued by the Treasury Task Force stress that the following conditions should first be satisfied:

- unequivocal commitment to the scheme and procurement via the PFI route by the project sponsor
- a fully costed public sector comparator or reference project which is affordable to the client and approved by all the relevant parties
- a statement of how the project will be funded over the life span of the contract
- criteria for longlisting and shortlisting bids
- a comprehensive risk allocation matrix
- establishing the team and appointment of advisers
- a draft output specification setting out the core requirements to be procured
- a draft of the basic terms and conditions of the contract with proposed performance measures, payment mechanism and risk allocation
- outline planning permission.

The last four preconditions deserve further elaboration.

Establishing the team and appointing advisers

The project team must be put together at an early stage. It is important to make sure that members of the team have the particular skills which are needed to deliver a successful project. The precise composition of the team will vary between projects and sectors, but experience from other schemes shows that the following skills are critical to the smooth running of a PFI procurement:

- a project sponsor or owner (chief executive or senior staff)
- a project team (membership includes senior representatives from clinical areas, direct care and clinical support services; clinical management, services departments, estates/facilities, finance, information management and technology (IM&T), personnel, project owner, non-executive director)
- the project team may be supported by internal and external

advisers. These are likely to include representatives of those responsible for policy or business strategy, service users or other relevant stakeholders, procurement specialists, financial advisers, legal advisers and technical experts – particularly architects and estates personnel.

In general, some members of the project team (most notably, financial and legal advisers) will need to be brought in from outside. It is important for the public sector client to use the right criteria for appointing external advisers and to comply with all relevant procurement law. Selection criteria should include knowledge of the PFI; risk allocation and assessment; knowledge of the sector in which advice is being sought (e.g. information technology); knowledge of the procurement process (including EC procurement law); and experience in providing practical advice to senior members in both the public and private sectors. Where appropriate, external advisers may be retained to provide advice when required and paid on a success fee basis.

A PFI procurement will normally require a swift and efficient decision-making process at the various stages. It is therefore important for lines of responsibility to be clearly defined, proper delegations and communication arrangements are in place, and the various members of the team are fully briefed so that they all speak with one voice.

Further tips on how to assemble the project team, select and manage advisers are provided in 5 *Steps to the Appointment of Advisers to PFI Projects* (Private Finance Panel May 1996).

Output-based specification

Work on the output-based specification (OBS) should be conducted in parallel with the development of the OBC. Detailed OBS must be developed both for the facilities and for each of the services for which bids will be sought from the private sector. These should cover the trust's service requirements (outputs, outcomes, as well as minimum quality and performance standards). The OBS must focus on what must be achieved to meet these requirements rather than how to achieve it. Stated alternatively, it must encourage innovation, high performance and improved cost-effectiveness.

To gain commitment to the project from managers, clinical staff, non-clinical staff and end users, it is important to involve all these stakeholders in producing the OBS. The main steps involved in preparing an OBS are:

- Stage 1 – define objectives and express these in terms of outputs (i.e. What is the service need? What is the organisation trying to achieve? If there are numerous needs, it may be helpful to bidders to rank these in priority order).
- Stage 2 – define the scope of the services or facilities covered by the OBS (specify what services are included and what are excluded, taking account of services at all of the trust's sites. Avoid defining how the services should be provided as this will inhibit the ability of the private sector to produce an innovative solution to meeting the client's requirement).
- Stage 3 – define minimum requirements for facilities and services (taking into account statutory requirements, Patient's Charter, requirements of end users, commissioners, good practice, access arrangements, the type of environment, the need to ensure flexibility in the design of the building to accommodate future expansion and contraction of services, functional relationships, functional content, etc.).
- Stage 4 – identify the constraints which may impinge on solutions offered by potential bidders (e.g. restrictions on planning permission, access to buildings, etc.).
- Stage 5 – to enable the bidder to develop an appropriate solution, an indication of the likely activity levels to be met should be provided (e.g. by providing relevant data on throughputs – number of in-patients, day cases and out-patients by specialty). In future, bidders will also be required to take into account the recommendations of the government's National Beds Inquiry which is currently under-way.
- Stage 6 – systems must be developed for measuring the performance of the contractor against the minimum requirements or service standards specified. This should be designed to:
  - provide an objective method of measuring performance
  - minimise the time and resources spent by the trust on monitoring
  - provide incentives to meet the minimum requirements.

Further tips on how to prepare an OBS is provided in *Writing an Output Specification* (Private Finance Panel October 1996).

It is important to recognise that developing sound OBSs is not a sufficient condition for delivering the desired outcome. The private sector must be able to respond to the procuring entity's requirements with cost-effective and innovative solutions. It has been argued in some quarters that the private sector does not, in some cases, possess the necessary expertise to meet this requirement. In the health sector, for example, Meara (1997) argues:

Most consortia members do not know enough about the technicalities of healthcare to argue the toss with clinicians and most are eager to show their ability to respond to requirements with innovative solutions. The result may be over-specified and over-engineered provision, sub-optimal space utilisation, a radical move away from the lower cost standard solutions of the 1970s and 1980s which were represented by the nucleus approach to building design and construction. [pp. 16–17]

There is some flaw in this argument. There is no incentive for the private sector to produce over-engineered and inefficient solutions since this would not augur well for value for money and affordability. In all probability, such schemes would not be approved. Departure from the nucleus approach to building hospitals is justifiable if the private sector is able to produce a better quality solution that reduces life cycle costs.

Another common misunderstanding is the argument raised in some quarters, most notably by Gaffney and Pollock (1997), that bed numbers are squeezed under PFI as a means of making such schemes affordable. Bed numbers under privately funded schemes are comparable with those under their public sector alternative. Under both approaches, bed numbers are reducing but for reasons that are unconnected with the way the scheme is funded. The reductions are being driven by changes in medical practices, discovery of new drugs, improvements in NHS performance (resulting in falls in average length of stay, increased day case rates, etc.), and other factors which influence demand for in-patient beds. The Calderdale case study in Chapter 7 sheds further light on the forces behind the declining numbers.

The contract framework

The draft contract structure should be regarded as a basis for negotiations. It should clearly indicate the trust's proposed approach to such essential elements of the deal as the length of the contract, risk transfer, payment mechanism, default events, termination events and protection for the trust in the event of the consortium or any of its members becoming insolvent. By presenting a contract structure from its perspective, the trust is able to stress those issues that are important to its own interests. The draft contract structure should not be presented as a *fait accompli*: it should be intended to serve as a basis for negotiations. Shortlisted bidders should be invited to comment on the draft contract before the Invitation to Negotiate (ITN) is formally issued.

In most PFI projects, the preferred bidder will be a consortium. The consortium members will typically form a new corporate entity to contract with the trust (the so-called 'special purpose vehicle' – SPV), which will subcontract with the consortium members and other service providers. Contracting with an SPV has the advantage of sourcing the complete range of services from one entity, with the SPV assuming responsibility for managing the subcontracts with private sector providers. Since the SPV is a newly established company, in general, it will not have any assets or liabilities other than those taken on for the project. The procurer should consider whether any members of the consortium should themselves be required to stand behind the SPV in providing guarantees or other forms of support.

The procurer will need to work closely with its legal and financial advisers in drafting the contract documents. These should reflect the fact that the contract will usually be for a full range of services over the whole life of the project, from the design and build stage through to the full operational phase. Each of these phases is likely to be covered by its own set of documents. Each document will specify for when and in what circumstances it is to become effective. The main documents typically include a **project agreement** (covering the construction and operational phases), a **development agreement** (covering the design, construction and commissioning of the new facility), a **services agreement** (describes the various services to be provided in the form of an output specification and proposed payment structure), a **headlease** and a **sublease**.

The project agreement will last for the whole duration of the contract and will cover issues such as:

- any conditions which must be satisfied before the project can proceed (e.g. obtaining finance)
- default events (definition and impact)
- *force majeure* events (definition and consequences)
- dispute resolution procedure
- termination events
- compensation provisions
- inspection and handback at the end of the contract
- SPV's insurance obligations
- indemnities
- procurement of collateral warranties.

Further details on what to specify in the contract framework are provided in a number of sources. These include NHSE's *PFI Manual* (1999) and the Treasury Task Force's guidance on *Standardisation of PFI Contracts* (1999). The Department of Health expect NHS bodies to adopt the standard terms and conditions contained in the model contract outlined in its *PFI Manual*. Any proposal to customise the standard contract should receive prior approval from the Department of Health.

Payment mechanisms

The payment mechanism for a scheme forms a vital part of the PFI contract. The client needs to have a clear understanding of the kind of mechanism it will accept before beginning the procurement. The payment mechanism also needs to be compatible with risk allocation and the flexibilities required of the scheme. It will also have a major bearing on the accounting treatment for the scheme.

The payment mechanism should be designed to satisfy the following objectives and principles:

- allocating risks to the party best able to manage them
- ensuring that the private sector genuinely assumes risk with potentially 100% variability of payments (based on the principle of no hospital, no fee)
- payment should only be for services received
- encouraging the private sector to deliver on time
- providing incentives for the private sector to deliver services that meet the agreed performance standards and improve their performance
- reward the private sector for efficiency savings
- making sure that the client is able to fulfil its financial obligations
- simplicity and transparency to make monitoring easy to implement.

The development of the payment mechanism should take into account factors such as indexation of the payment stream throughout the contract period to take account of inflation, and the market testing or benchmarking of services. It should be structured so as to allow the client to recover VAT which is charged on the services provided under the PFI contract.

Outline planning permission and statutory consultation

Outline planning permission for the scheme should be obtained before it is advertised. However, it should be recognised that bidders may suggest the use of alternative sites or solutions which will render the original planning permission nugatory. Bids which are within the original planning permission are not necessarily more advantageous than those which necessitate new outline planning permission. The costs and benefits of the additional time delay posed by the latter should be considered carefully.

Statutory consultation about the scheme should also be completed before the *Official Journal of the European Community* (OJEC) notice is issued. This will render the scheme more attractive to potential bidders. Chapter 7 provides lessons from the Calderdale NHS Trust's scheme on how to involve the Community Health Council (CHC) and other stakeholders in the planning and execution of a major capital scheme or service reconfiguration.

Market soundings

Taking soundings within the relevant market before the project has been formally advertised may be necessary to gauge interest in the project. For schemes with a capital cost above £25m, this could be done at the SOC stage. Feedback from this process could be used to inform the development of the SOC and the PFI ability assessment for the scheme. It is important for this exercise to be conducted in a manner which does not prejudice the subsequent procurement process. Legal advice should be sought before approaching the market.

Although this is not a mandatory requirement, for it to be useful, the exercise should be planned carefully and approached systematically. The public sector body should address issues such as:

- Who are the suppliers in the market at present?
- Is the market fully developed?
- Is there surplus capacity in the market to undertake the project?
- Which suppliers should be approached?
- How should they be approached?
- What action should be taken to avoid breaching the procurement regulations?
- How should the results from the exercise be used?
- How should the project proceed if the results show it is unlikely to be viable as a PFI project?

Conclusion

It has been argued in a number of quarters that the NHS won the 'contest' for being the worst performing sector for PFI in 1996. None of the big hospital deals was clinched. As we have seen in this chapter, this is no longer the case. In fact, few, if any, would disagree that the NHS has been the best performing area for PFI in 1997 and 1998. This is set to continue in 1999.

The NHS's experience underlines the importance of:

- rational planning of schemes based on service priorities and deliverability
- close collaboration between all the relevant local, regional and national stakeholders in the planning of schemes
- close attention to be paid to affordability and for this assessment to factor in the cost of risks and all the other factors which have a bearing on the viability of projects
- securing the PFI market and responding appropriately to the concerns of financiers and other partners involved in these transactions
- proper preparation before commencing the procurement.

Public sector organisations contemplating PFI procurements should not underestimate the amount of effort and resources required to produce OBSs, draft contract terms and conduct other preparatory activities.

CHAPTER THREE

Managing the PFI procurement process

As noted in the previous chapter, good, all-round preparation is crucial to running a successful PFI procurement. The other key ingredient for obtaining the desired outcome is a sound knowledge of the procurement process and the relevant procurement regulations.

This chapter provides an overview of the procurement process from OJEC advertisement to contract award, and provides a number of practical tips for managing the process to produce better and speedier procurements. It also emphasises the need for openness, fairness and transparency – the key hallmarks of the European Community procurement regime. Chapters 7 and 8 provide two case studies based on the procurement model discussed in this chapter.

Awareness of procurement regulations

The Treasury Task Force's booklet *A Step-by-Step Guide to the PFI Process*, first published in July 1997 and updated in April 1998, remains the most authoritative source on the stages involved in a typical PFI procurement. Two other useful sources are Morrison and Owen (1996) and Cirrel *et al.* (1997). This chapter draws primarily from these three sources to outline the PFI procurement process.

The procurer needs to have a good working knowledge of the relevant procurement regulations (or have access to advice from procurement lawyers), the likely timescale and costs of the procurement, and the role which internal and external advisers should play in the process. The procuring body should note that even the appointment of advisers may fall within the orbit of the procurement regulations. This should be taken into account when assessing the timescale and cost of the procurement. The risk of legal challenge from aggrieved bidders who may have incurred substantial tendering costs should also be borne in mind.

Public sector organisations that are undertaking PFI projects should conform to all relevant procurement regulations. They should also conduct a proper audit of the process they have followed.

The relevant UK procurement regulations which apply to PFI schemes are:

• Public Works Contracts Regulations 1991 (SI 1991/2680)
• Public Services Contracts Regulations 1993 (SI 1993/3228)
• Public Supply Contracts Regulations 1995 (SI 1995/201).

These regulations enact EC directives under UK law. The regulations apply to contracts with a value over the following thresholds:

• Public Works £4 016 744
• Public Services £104 435
• Public Supply £104 425.

These thresholds have been in place since 1 January 1998. They are updated every two years.

Intuition would suggest that the services-oriented nature of PFI contracts would make them fall under the 'Public Services' directive. However, such projects are often very capital-intensive and could also fall under the 'Public Works' category. The ambiguity is reflected in the following passage from the Central Unit of Procurement Guidance Note 51:

> In most cases the classification of contracts will be straight-forward. The Regulations provided that where a contract covers both services and supplies, including any siting and installation of the goods, the classification should be determined by the respective values of the two elements . . . There is no . . . value-based formula for determining into which category a mixed works/supplies or works/services contract falls. In such cases the contract should be classified according to its predominant purpose (cited in Cirell *et al.* 1997, pp. B3.13–14).

It is important for the procuring entity to seek sound legal advice to ensure their procurement conforms fully with these regulations. It is good practice to include a copy of this opinion in the business case.

Contracts may be awarded under any of three procedures – open, restricted and negotiated. Under the 'open procedure' there is no pre-qualification stage and any number of contractors can respond to the

OJEC notice. Under the 'restricted procedure' the client can confine discussions to a sample of those suppliers who have responded to the OJEC notice. However, such discussions are limited to issues of clarification rather than meaningful negotiation. Under the negotiated procedure, however, both of these drawbacks are avoided. The client is allowed to pre-qualify bidders and conduct detailed negotiations with those who satisfy the project requirements.

The negotiated procedure is thus the recommended route for PFI projects. Clients should note, however, that they do not have an automatic right to use this procedure. A justification should be provided for using the negotiated procedure.

Overview of the PFI process

Once the OBC has been approved and the preparatory work described in the previous section has been completed, formal procurement can begin. The Treasury Task Force guidance, *Step-by-Step Guide to the PFI Process* (1997), identifies 14 stages in the PFI procurement process. This is outlined in Figure 3.1. This figure has been adapted to show how these stages relate to the business case process. The ensuing exposition summarises the main features of what the author sees as the key stages. No attempt is made to reiterate the details in the Treasury Task Force's model.

Timescales

The timescale for completing the whole process will depend on a number of factors, most notably, the size and type of project, the complexity of the project, the commitment of the project team, the quality of advisers (particularly legal and financial advisers), and the award procedure adopted. In the case of procurement of a major hospital scheme, assuming the recommendations of the PFI review are successfully implemented, the process from despatching the OJEC notice to contract award is expected to last 18 months on average.

This contrasts with three years for most of the tranche 1 schemes, and reflects the various reforms which the Department of Health and Treasury Task Force have introduced since May 1997. The main stages with indicative timetable is shown in Box 3.1. This assumes the

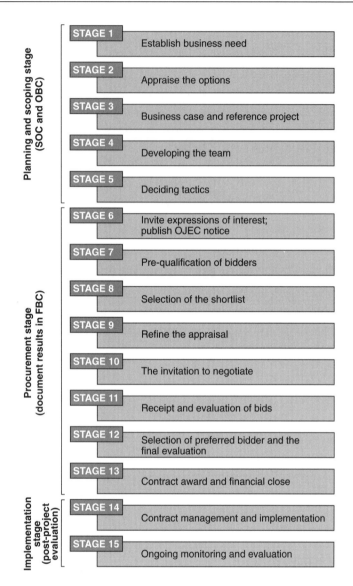

Figure 3.1: The PFI procurement process (adapted from Treasury Task Force, April 1998).

preliminary ITNs are issued to a longlist of bidders following pre-qualification. It is obviously too early to assess the realism of this timescale. Although largely based on the processes in place prior to the PFI Review, the case studies in Chapters 7 and 8 suggest this may be difficult to achieve, especially for schemes with complex designs and a large number of stakeholders. It will also depend on the amount and

Box 3.1: Milestones and indicative timetable for major projects

Milestone	Duration (days)
OJEC notice	1
Deadline for expressions of interest	37
Deadline for pre-qualification	28
Evaluation of pre-qualification submissions and longlist of up to six	21
Deadline for response to preliminary ITN	60
Evaluation of response and shortlist of three	21
Deadline for fully priced bids to preliminary ITN	60
Evaluation down to two	21
Negotiations with two	56
Deadline for fixed price bids	28
Evaluation down to one	21
Negotiating leading up to FBC submission	77
FBC approval	90
Financial close	30
Total	approximately 18 months

quality of resources the stakeholders (including the PFU) are able to commit to the project.

Publish contract notice in OJEC

Transparency and fairness are key features of the EC procurement regulations. Public sector bodies are, therefore, required to publicise the contract notice in the OJEC. If advertisements are placed in other media (e.g. specialist press), these should not appear before the OJEC version has been despatched and should not contain any information additional to what is in the OJEC. The required format of the contract notice is described in the relevant directive.

The advertisement should contain all the necessary information about the project to enable bidders to respond appropriately to the clients' requirements. It should stress that a PFI solution is being sought and that 'variant bids' are acceptable. The criteria which will be used to evaluate potential bidders' commercial standing and technical capacity should be indicated. The advertisement should also state which procurement procedure will be used to take the project forward. As previously indicated, the negotiated procedure will generally be used for PFI procurement as it provides flexibility to the client.

Examples of OJEC advertisements for a hospital building project and an IM&T project are provided in Chapters 7 and 8. Further guidance on how to draft an OJEC advertisement may be found in *How To Follow EC Procurement Procedure and Advertise in the OJEC* (HM Treasury Task Force 1998).

Under the negotiated procedure route, interested bidders are allowed at least 37 days to indicate an interest in undertaking the work. They may be expected to request a pre-qualification questionnaire and an outline specification of the project. They may also wish to visit the procuring authority's premises. These requests should be anticipated.

Pre-qualification of bidders

All parties who express an interest in the project should be sent an 'Information Memorandum' and a pre-qualification questionnaire. These should be designed to elicit information for judging whether potential bidders are technically and financially capable of satisfying the requirements of the project.

The respondents to the OJEC who have notified their interest on receipt of these documents and who have submitted the required information should be reduced to a manageable shortlist or longlist, based on suitable and credible criteria. Regulation 14 of the procurement laws provides some of the grounds for preliminary elimination of bidders or consortium members. Bidders who have criminal convictions relating to the conduct of their business, bankruptcy, failure to pay social security contributions, etc. are automatically disqualified.

The information that should be taken into account in assessing bidders' commercial and technical standing is set out in the relevant procurement regulation. Supplementary information may be requested under the circumstances specified in Regulation 17. Factors relating to the award of the contract itself (e.g. any innovation proposed by the bidder) should not be taken into account at this stage. Such factors should be considered at the ITN stage just as factors relating to the commercial and technical standing of the bidders should not normally be considered at the ITN stage. The sifting process should be open, fair and transparent.

Selection of the shortlist

As noted before, pre-qualification is a test of general commercial and technical suitability to meet the requirements of the project. To short-list from those who pre-qualify, suitable tests should be devised to ascertain the bidders' ability and commitment to offer an affordable fit-for-purpose bid. These tests should consider factors such as the technical approach which bidders would bring to the project, their capacity and appetite to assume risk, how they propose to finance the project, and indicative price. Pricing at this stage should be approached with care since the OBS is not likely to be finalised at this stage. Pre-qualified bidders whose bids are rejected at this stage should be debriefed quickly.

The EC rejection/selection criteria and the commercial and technical information provide a sift for evaluating tenderers' potential to deliver the project. Firms with the most relevant expertise and experience are the ones who should be selected to proceed further.

Refine the project appraisal and output-based specification

This stage is an important precursor for issuing the Invitation to Negotiate (or Invitation to Tender). It is important to refine the OBS and any PSC in light of the knowledge gained from the procurement to date. In particular, the affordability of the scheme and funding commitments should be reaffirmed. This provides a sound basis to enable bidders to formulate viable bids to satisfy the project requirements.

The invitation to negotiate

The ITN provides the framework for the pre-qualified bidders to develop their detailed bids. Considerable care needs to be taken to ensure it is comprehensive, accurate and clearly drafted. Apart from enabling bidders to develop accurate proposals, it should be designed to elicit the information on which the client will need to compare bids, including comparison of private sector bids against the PSC.

Practice varies between departments in terms of how they handle this phase. The latest guidance from the Department of Health outlines two alternative routes which are acceptable from NHS organisations:

1 they can either longlist up to six bidders (based on the results of the pre-qualification exercise) and issue a preliminary ITN to them. From their response to the preliminary ITN, they should then shortlist three bidders and issue the final ITN to them; or
2 they can shortlist three bidders (based on the pre-qualification) and issue the Final ITN to them.

Initial responses should be sought from the three shortlisted bidders arising from either route. Following evaluation and initial negotiations of these responses, this list should be reduced to two bidders from whom detailed bids should be sought. After evaluation of the final bids, a preferred bidder should be appointed. The other bidder should be given 'reserve status' and will be required to re-enter the competition if a value-for-money deal cannot be negotiated with the preferred bidder.

To obtain the desired outcome, bidders must be provided with relevant information about the project. The ITN is likely to address issues such as those indicated in Box 3.2. Bidders should be invited to submit information on the following key areas:

- support for the procuring entity's service philosophy and objectives
- proposed services approach (e.g. method statements relating to key aspects of the output specifications, quality assurance arrangements, arrangements for managing the interface between clinical and non-clinical services, etc.)
- proposed approach to design (e.g. likely type of design solution, illustrations and narrative to demonstrate the design philosophy and the steps which will be taken to make the facility inherently flexible and adaptable to cope with changes in service requirements, etc.)
- proposed construction approach (e.g. broad balance between new build and refurbishment, indicative construction timetable, phasing and decanting arrangements, etc.)
- proposed method of funding the scheme (e.g. likely sources of finance, expectations of debt maturity, interest rates, margins, cover ratios, etc.)
- confirmation that they and consortium members accept the proposed risk allocation and the standard contract
- how they propose to meet the requirements for information technology and equipment
- how issues such as surplus land and anything specific to the scheme

Box 3.2: Examples of what to include in the ITN for an NHS capital scheme

- Details of the project sponsors (NHS trust's business objectives, current configuration of services, activity and performance information, NHS trust's catchment area, its position in the local health economy, most recent income and expenditure accounts, and sources of its income, etc.)
- Details of the commissioning health authoritiy or PCG(s) (commissioner's business objectives, current and future commissioning intentions, management structure, etc.)
- Details of the project (scheme objectives, functional content, list of non-clinical services to be provided under the contract, etc.)
- Output specifications (for facilities, each of the non-clinical services to be provided under the contract, and those services – clinical and non-clinical – which the trust will continue to provide, etc.)
- Affordability envelope within which bids should be contained (including underlying assumptions)
- Contract structure (summary of contractural terms governing the project, desired contract length, statement of any areas of the contract which are non-negotiable, draft project agreement and supporting schedules, etc.). The Department's standard contract should be adopted (*see PFI Manual* (NHSE 1999))
- Allocation of risks (description of allocation of risks, risk matrix reflecting the draft contract, details of any specific risks which are non-negotiable)
- Payment mechanism (structure of payment mechanism, performance monitoring regime, proposed method of indexation, market testing or benchmarking arrangements)
- Land and buildings (details of existing land and buildings, details of any surplus land available, details of any existing planning permissions, etc.)
- Bidders' financial strategy (details of how the project will be funded, proposed shareholders, format of proposed financial model, details of assumptions underlying the financial model, etc.)
- Timetable (from submission of bids to delivery of services, statement of minimum period for which prices of fixed bids must be held prior to financial close)
- Equipment and IM&T strategy (summary of equipment and IM&T strategy, details of equipment and IM&T to be provided under the scheme, etc.)

will be addressed (e.g. are there any opportunities for generating income from third parties?)
• commitment to provide a full financial model to represent their bid in a format specified by the procuring entity.

The degree of commitment expected from bidders will vary with the stage they are at in the ITN process. At the preliminary ITN stage, all three bidders are required to:

• confirm acceptance of the key clauses outlined in the contract structure
• confirm whether the proposed contract terms are likely to be acceptable to their subcontractors and financiers
• outline their approach to meeting the requirements set out in the OBS.

At the final ITN stage, the two remaining bidders are required to:

• reach 'outline agreement' with the procuring entity on all key contractual issues, particularly those affecting the tariff, risk allocation, and payment mechanism
• produce 1:500 drawings, sketch plans, selected blow-ups, functional relationships between departments, floor plans for clinical areas and outline area schedule
• confirm acceptance of standard contract, payment mechanism, risk allocation and performance regime
• develop full financial model to represent their bid
• confirm support from financiers and their acceptance of the contract terms, financial model, risk allocation, payment mechanism and performance regime
• confirm and identify all the members of the consortium.

Before selecting the preferred partner, agreement should be reached on all contractual issues which have a bearing on the tariff and risk allocation. A credible set of evaluation criteria should be used throughout the ITN stage. This should focus on both the quantitative and qualitative aspects of the bids (see next section).

Discussions with bidders during the tender period should be encouraged as this allows bidders to gain a better understanding of the client's requirements. If these discussions lead to any modification to the scope of the project, such changes should be communicated to all bidders.

The negotiating team need to have a clear negotiating strategy before the actual negotiations begin. This should be clearly understood by each member of the team so that they all work professionally towards the same goal. This stage is likely to be very lengthy for major projects – perhaps three or four months. There is a lot of material for bidders to absorb in order to be able to formulate and prepare a formal bid.

The discussions should focus on the commercial terms of the contract, and ensuring that the project will be delivered cost-effectively. More specific objectives include:

- to ensure each bidder fully understands the public sector's service requirements
- to ensure the public sector is clear on the solution that is being proposed
- to ensure the prices are robust and any proposed solution is bankable
- to ensure the responsibilities of both parties are clearly understood and reflected in the documentation developed
- to satisfy all PFI policy requirements (optimal risk allocation, contract structure test, etc.)
- to identify and resolve all potentially contentious issues (e.g. limits of liability)
- to identify the best value-for-money bid (taking into account quality, achievability, realism and affordability).

Receipt and evaluation of bids

The aim of this stage is to compare the costs and benefits of each bid in order to identify the most economically advantageous PFI proposal. The assessment of benefits should take risk transfer into account and both quantitative and qualitative benefits. The latter group of benefits should include human resource issues such as Transfer of Undertakings (Protection of Employment) Regulations 1981 (TUPE), pay, working conditions and staff management.

Different bidders will offer different solutions to the client's requirements. It is therefore important for these solutions to be evaluated fairly and objectively. Bidders will have already been informed of the evaluation criteria at earlier stages in the process, particularly the ITN stage.

If the client proposes to award the contract on the basis of economic advantage, this should be based on the factors in the relevant procurement Regulations. Regulation 20 of the Public Works Contracts Regulations 1991 lists these as price, period for completion, running costs, profitability and technical merit. For services (*see* Regulation 21 of the Public Services Contracts Regulations 1993), they include period for completion or delivery, quality, aesthetic and functional characteristics, technical merit, after-sales service, technical assistance and price.

Other evaluation criteria may be added to the list if they are relevant to the performance of the contract and to assessing best value for money. Factors to consider include quality of the design solution, capital costs, risk allocation, proposed tariff/value for money, contractual terms and duration, affordability, payment mechanism, flexibilities to cope with changing requirements, human resource issues, cultural compatibility and other non-financial factors. The importance of qualitative criteria should not be downplayed. 'Soft' criteria such as the 'culture' and 'values' of the bidders will have an important bearing on long-term *partnership* arrangements.

The evaluation of the bids is usually undertaken by the team which has undertaken the negotiations. It is important to ensure that legal, financial and technical advisers contribute to this crucial stage.

Once the evaluation criteria have been agreed, weights should be assigned to the criteria to reflect their relative importance. A scoring system should also be devised (see Chapters 5, 7 and 8 for practical examples). It is good practice to discuss the evaluation model with all shortlisted bidders before it is finalised. The model should also be applied consistently and even-handedly to evaluate each bid.

Sensitivity analysis should be performed to demonstrate the impact of changes in key variables on the net present value (NPV) or any weighted scores produced for each bid. The evaluation model needs to be robust and credible.

Selection of the preferred bidder

This is a crucial stage in the procurement process. The requirement in the health sector is for the terms of the contract to be developed to an advanced stage with two shortlisted bidders before a preferred bidder is selected. It will require considerable resources and time to undertake two sets of negotiations simultaneously. The client will need to balance the costs to both itself and the private sector of conducting two sets of negotiations and the benefits which result from maintaining competition for longer.

Before selecting the preferred bidder the client should satisfy itself that the PFI proposal is affordable and passes the value-for-money test. This will require a robust and up-to-date PSC. However, the revision of the PSC should not mimic any design, engineering or operational attributes offered by the private sector (see Chapter 5). The shortlisted bidders should have:

- agreed all key contract terms (including agreement from financiers)
- developed a full, audited financial model to represent the project
- confirmed with financiers draft term sheets for funding the project (including confirmation of their acceptance of all key contract terms, financial model, payment mechanism and proposed risk allocation)
- submitted their best and final offers
- ensured their bids fall within the client's stipulated affordability envelope
- agreed to absorb all price changes other than those resulting from interest rates.

The client should also ensure that the private sector's PFI solution is bankable and that financiers are appropriately involved. Financiers should be appointed carefully. The terms on which they provide funding will have a major bearing on the cost of the PFI solution, hence the value-for-money test. It is also important to ensure financiers are knowledgable about the procuring entity's business environment (i.e. knowledge of the particular sector) and are willing to accept the proposed contract terms and desired risk allocation. Experience of funding PFI projects would also be an advantage.

It is good practice for the public sector client to meet each shortlisted bidder's proposed financiers (funders and third party equity providers) before selecting the two shortlisted bidders. By this stage financiers should provide written support and draft term sheets to confirm their support for the scheme. In particular, they should confirm acceptance of all key contract terms, the payment mechanism, performance regime, financial model and the risks allocated to the consortium.

Before providing this commitment financiers, in turn, will need to beg'n their due diligence work and satisfy themselves on all of the fundamental aspects of the transaction. In the case of schemes within the health sector, the due diligence work typically covers issues such as:

- the quality of the NHS trust's management team
- the way the trust and commissioning health authority or PCG is funded and their financial stability
- the business and purchasing strategy of the various NHS organisations involved in the transaction
- the risks inherent in the project, their allocation and the capabilities of the parties to manage the risks allocated to them.

When the preferred bidder has been chosen, it is good practice to retain the remaining bidder as a 'reserve'. The reserve bidder may re-enter the negotiations if an acceptable deal cannot be reached with the preferred bidder. This helps to exert competitive pressures on the process.

Contract award and financial close

If the correct procedures have been used to select the preferred and reserve bidders, the process to contract award and financial close should be straightforward. By this stage, the preferred bidder, its subcontractors and financiers will have accepted the key commercial terms of the deal and the project documentation. The members of the consortium will have agreed to the risks allocated to them by accepting the heads of terms for the subcontractors and the financing agreements. Financiers will have completed initial due diligence. In short, there should be few (if any) commercial issues of substance to be addressed after the preferred bidder is selected. However, considerable work will still remain at this stage; particularly negotiations on the details of the contract and any issues raised in the due diligence process, the drafting of contract schedules, financing and other documentation. Ambiguities and omissions of relevant clauses should be avoided in the drafting as these are frequently the source of disputes and claims.

Before the contract is awarded, a Full Business Case summarising all material aspects of the deal should be submitted to the NHS Executive and HM Treasury for approval. The key requirements and content of the FBC is discussed in Chapter 6. Once the scheme has been approved, immediately before financial close, the NHS Executive will undertake a further review of the project to ensure it still satisfies the approval criteria. In line with the government's policy on openness, the NHS trust will be required to publish an addendum to the FBC within one month of financial close. Once the contract has been awarded, the client is required to place a contract award notice in the OJEC within 48 days of awarding the contract.

Contract management

This is a distinct phase which follows on from the procurement process. The procurement process is a means to an end. The client will need to put mechanisms in place to ensure the facility is completed on time and to the required standard, and that the level of services delivered over the life span of the contract fully meets the standards laid down in the OBS and the relevant contract documentation. The client will need to appoint someone with the appropriate expertise to monitor compliance with the contract during the various phases of the project.

The monitoring arrangements should be designed to:

- measure the contractor's performance and be based on a fair, objective and transparent system
- respond to change control requirements throughout the life of the contract
- provide management information to gauge value for money and test the original assumptions in the case, particularly those relating to risks.

The PFI process for information services and technology (IS/IT) projects

The procurement process discussed above is generic. However, it is worth noting there are a number of special considerations arising from IS/IT projects, which require suitable adaptation of the approach depicted in this chapter. The most notable distinguishing features are:

- Unlike the majority of PFI deals where the asset outlasts the deal, the situation is reversed with IS/IT projects. The average duration of the contract is 7–10 years, during which time there would normally be at least one upgrading of the technology.
- IS/IT projects can directly influence core business processes in the public sector, such as the processing of immigration cases or the payment of social security benefits.
- IS/IT projects, if scoped properly, can provide opportunities for the complete re-engineering of business processes.
- IS/IT deals are usually measured and paid for through cost savings or increased efficiencies but they will normally have a higher service

content than other types of PFI projects. Note, however, that this is not intended to gainsay the importance of non-financial benefits.

- The design and implementation of IS/IT projects are particularly complex. Unlike a half-finished construction project which has a fixed value attached to it, the worth to financiers of an incomplete IT system or a system that does not work is effectively nil. Financiers are wary about lending large sums of money for such projects until they have been developed and offer the potential to generate revenue.
- IS/IT will include provisions for dealing with intellectual property rights and continuity of the IS/IT skills needed to deliver the requirements of the contract (Central IT Unit 1998, p. 2).

Given these distinguishing features, special consideration should be given to whether to procure IS/IT services as part of the main contract for the provision of hospital or other services. This decision should be made before the project is advertised. Much will depend on the role of IS/IT in the scoping of the project and the delivery of the desired benefits. The procuring entity will need to ensure it acts in full compliance with the relevant EU and departmental regulations. As with other aspects of the procurement, close attention should also be paid to value for money and affordability in deciding on how best to procure IS/IT services.

Conclusion

This chapter has outlined the main stages involved in a PFI procurement. While it is no substitute for first-hand experience of the process itself, it should, nevertheless, alert procurers to what to expect and how best to prepare for the procurement. In addition, it is recommended that they consult other relevant public sector bodies about their experience of undertaking PFI procurements. Chapters 7 and 8 provide two case studies based on the procurement model discussed in this chapter.

Based on lessons learned from undertaking PFI procurements to date, the following tips should be noted:

- careful planning of the various stages of the procurement process is essential to obtain the desired outcome
- ensure the project is properly scoped with no unnecessary constraints being placed on potential suppliers
- IS/IT services are difficult and complex to organise (especially when

they are included as part of a major capital scheme) and require special attention
- establish a well-balanced and experienced project team. Ensure the relevant advisers are brought in at the right stage
- manage advisers and their fees carefully. Poor advice, sometimes obtained at extortionate costs, has been a major reason for a number of the failed or abortive PFI projects
- be clear about the procurement rules and ensure these are followed in spirit and letter
- ensure evaluation criteria are relevant, credible and based on specialist advice
- maintain a clear and comprehensive audit trail of the process followed at each stage of the procurement
- be sensitive to the needs of bidders and avoid imposing unnecessary bidding costs on them
- be clear about the inter-relationship between the business case process and the procurement process. Both processes are interdependent
- remember that competition is ultimately the best guarantor of value for money.

CHAPTER 4

The assessment and management of risks

Risk is the possibility of different outcomes arising from a decision. Such a possibility is inherent in all projects, regardless of how they are financed. In PFI transactions, risk is far from being just another 'four-letter word' which can be ignored. Optimal risk allocation is one of the cornerstones of the policy. Its centrality is reflected in every piece of guidance which has been produced to aid implementation of the policy. Risk has a direct bearing on the value-for-money analysis, affordability, accounting treatment, the contract terms and, ultimately, the success or otherwise of the project. Procurers are therefore required to consider and assess risk throughout the whole PFI process: from inception of the project to contract award and throughout the operating period.

This chapter explains the role of risk in PFI transactions, the types of risk which are associated with such transactions, techniques for identifying and assessing risks, risk management strategies and how risk should be addressed in business cases. It concludes with a list of pitfalls to avoid when conducting a risk analysis.

Understanding the perspectives of the different parties

As noted before, optimal risk allocation is one of the mantras which continue to dominate PFI. It is an area which is closely scrutinised by public watchdog bodies and those who are directly involved in approving the deal. As the NAO noted in 1996:

Although the NAO's investigative work on PFI projects has just begun, it is quite clear that a key issue will be the way PFI projects handle risk: who bears what risks, how much risk traditionally borne by the public sector is transferred to the private sector, and at what price. Consistent with my attitude of welcoming well thought out innovations, the NAO will be looking for thorough analysis of risks in PFI projects. (House of Commons Treasury Committee 1996)

All the parties involved in a PFI transaction will need to undertake a risk analysis. Typically, there are three groups of players: the public sector client, the private sector bidder and the financiers. Although the methodology adopted to identify and assess risks is likely to be common, the parties are likely to have different objectives. It is instructive to note their respective interests in risk analysis.

The public sector will need to satisfy the risk transfer guidelines laid down in official guidance produced by the Treasury Task Force and other bodies involved in PFI policy-making. It will need to be able to assess the magnitude of risk each competing bidder is prepared to assume during the bid evaluation process. It will also need to demonstrate it has identified and allocated risk optimally (i.e. to the party who is best placed to manage it).

The private sector will need to consider whether (and how) it can manage the risks which the public sector has earmarked for transfer. This will include considerations such as whether such risks can be further allocated to its subcontractors and other members of the consortium. It will also need to price all risks it assumes and those it has decided to manage through insurance arrangements. It will need to ensure that any risk assumed is *bankable* and acceptable to financiers. The risks should be allocated and priced in such a way that they do not distort the project economics and create a misalignment between net project revenue and debt service. Unlike equity investors who are looking for a long-term return through dividend or interest on subordinated debt, banks will be more risk averse and will generally be looking for a return of principal and payment of interest and fees over a shorter time frame.

The project financiers will need to ensure that the allocation of risk between the public and private sectors (and within the private sector) is appropriate. It will need to be satisfied that all the parties have effective mechanisms in place to manage and absorb the potential financial consequences of the risks which they assume. This is particularly important since the SPV undertaking the project will be a 'shell' company, highly geared with limited capitalisation and assets other than its rights under the contract with the procuring entity.

Apart from examining the allocation of risks between the various parties, financiers will conduct extensive due diligence into the project, the vires and capacity of the awarding authority to support effective delivery of the project, and the market and political environment in which the project operates. The factors which influence revenue and the sensitivities of the variables which drive the project financial model will also be of special interest. It will also negotiate 'step in' or 'takeover' agreements in circumstances where any of the parties to the contract have committed a major breach which undermines the economics of the project. Collateral warranties and parent company guarantees will also be sought from subcontractors to provide additional comfort to financiers.

Risk analysis

Risk analysis is therefore important to all the parties involved in a PFI transaction. A risk assessment should be approached systematically and should be conducted both at the inception of the project and throughout its life cycle. It is not a one-off activity. The process entails four basic steps: (i) identification and definition, (ii) assessment and quantification, (iii) allocation, and (iv) management. These are discussed in turn.

Identification and definition

There are four major sources of risks:

- those factors which fall within an organisation's control
- those which are within the control of others with whom the organisation is forced to interact, for example the planning authority
- those which result from government regulation, for example changes in planning regulations and taxation
- those factors that are beyond the organisation's control, for example the weather.

The type of risks associated with a PFI scheme will depend on the nature of the particular project. Experience from schemes approved in the health sector suggests that in most cases, the following risks are likely to apply to major construction schemes:

- **design risk** – risks related to ensuring the asset is fit for its intended purpose
- **construction and development risk** – costs of not being able to provide the services by the agreed date and within the budget set by the project company
- **availability and performance risk** – the services (including facilities) provided not being available or up to the standard specified
- **operating cost risk** – the risk of fluctuating operating costs
- **variability of revenue risk** – level of service being significantly different from that planned with a resultant impact on the payments to the project company
- **termination risk** – the procuring body exercising its rights to step in and make alternative arrangements for the provision of the service
- **technology and obsolescence risk** – possibility of the underlying asset becoming an inefficient way of providing the required service because of technological changes
- **control risk** – the procuring body having such a level of influence over the way the project company delivers the services that it inhibits the ability of the project company to influence its own operating costs
- **residual value risk** – the allocation of the asset/liability associated with the residual value of the underlying asset at the end of the contract period
- **other project risks** – risks not covered under the above categories (e.g. uncertainty over the timing and value of capital receipts from the sale of surplus land or assets).

This list is adapted from the classification set out in the Audit Commission's guidance to auditors of NHS bodies (TR 37/96). It is also consistent with the guidance in the Department of Health's latest guidance to project sponsors in the NHS (NHSE 1999).

The particular risks under each of these categories are likely to be scheme-specific. Typically, several hundred risks are identified under the various categories. Their relative importance will also vary between schemes. It is important to identify the risks under each category systematically and comprehensively. The risks should also be clearly and unambiguously defined.

In the case of information services and technology projects, Box 4.1 provides a checklist of the key risk areas which should be considered. The list is consistent with the risks identified for construction schemes. There are a number of techniques which may be used to identify the risks which apply to the project. Three commonly used methods are:

- **Structured review meetings with the project team.** This encourages

---

Box 4.1: Checklist of risks for IS/IT projects (*see also* pp 170–2)

Design and build
- initial cost estimates
- design and construction timescales
- meeting specified requirements
- change management

Finance
- availability of finance

Commissioning and operating
- operational control
- commissioning timescale
- operating costs
- availability of service
- service performance
- change management

Service demand
- service capacity
- usage (volume/demand)

Technology or obsolescence
- assets become redundant
- refreshment and incentivisation

Regulatory
- change of law
- enabling legislations

---

participation and ownership by all key staff and external stakeholders. Effective facilitation and frank feedback are essential if the risks are to be comprehensively identified and realistically assessed. At this stage, assessment could focus on whether the relevant risks are likely to have a low, medium or high probability and financial impact.
- **Risk audit interviews.** These interviews should be conducted by experienced managers or advisers. The interviewers should interview all those who have experience of the risks surrounding the particular project. For example, if the project is an information technology scheme, then the interviews should be with people who have knowledge and/or experience of such projects. This method is particularly useful when there are large numbers of people involved

---

Box 4.2: Agenda for risk workshop

1 Introduction (objectives of workshop, scope of workshop, ground rules for workshop, questions and answers)
2 Roles of the participants
3 Introduction to the scheme (participants should be provided with all relevant information about the scheme at least two days before the workshop)
4 Risk identification and definition (establish the preliminary risk register, develop a risk allocation matrix – i.e. identify how the risks might be allocated between the public and private sector or other relevant parties)
5 Risk assessment and qualitative analysis (taking into account likely probability and financial consequences; rank the risk in terms of low, medium and high)
6 Risk assessment and quantitative analysis (assess whether the risks are quantifiable, identify data sources for all quantifiable risks, where possible provide preliminary estimate of likely probability and cost of each risk, select curve type)

---

in the project and where it is difficult to bring everyone together (e.g. because of problems of logistics).

- **Brainstorming workshops.** This is a facilitated workshop with members of the project team. The group will brainstorm all the risks that may apply to the project. These should subsequently be analysed so that all the material ones can be considered further. A typical agenda for such a workshop should address the issues indicated in Box 4.2.

Force majeure, compensation and relief events

Before discussing the assessment and quantification of risks, it is instructive to distinguish between three categories of 'delay events' which are likely to feature in a risk analysis. They are *force majeure*, compensation and relief events.

Force majeure events may arise at any stage during the life of the contract. They are usually shared as, even though they could have a catastrophic impact on the project, they are beyond the control of the parties to the contract. They typically include:

- war, civil war, armed conflict or terrorist attack arising within and/or affecting the UK

- nuclear, chemical or biological contamination arising from war and any of the other events mentioned above
- ionising radiation or contamination by radioactivity from any nuclear fuel or nuclear waste
- radioactive, toxic, explosive or other hazardous properties of any explosive nuclear assembly or component
- pressure waves caused by aircraft or other aerial devices travelling at sonic or supersonic speed.

Other events which cannot be insured at reasonable commercial rates may also be treated as *force majeure.*

Compensation events normally arise before the operational phase of the project and are usually borne by the procuring entity. Typically, they have the effect of delaying the commencement of the service, hence the contractor's revenue stream and its ability to repay its debt. They include events such as:

- a breach by the procuring entity of its obligations under the contract, but one which would not normally result in 'default' on the contract
- a change to the service initiated by the procuring entity
- discriminatory or specific change of law.

Relief events have the effect of preventing the contractor from performing its obligations and can arise at any time during the contract. The contractor bears the full financial consequences of such events, but is given relief from termination for failure to provide the full service. They include events such as:

- fire, explosion, lightning, storm, tempest, flood, bursting or overflowing water tanks, apparatus or pipes, earthquakes, riot and civil commotion
- the failure by a statutory undertaker, utility company, local authority or other like body to carry out works or provide services
- any accidental loss or damage to the site, the facility or any road servicing it
- any failure or shortage of power, fuel or transport
- any blockade or embargo which does not constitute *force majeure*
- the presence of an unexploded bomb or other ammunition
- any strikes, lockout, go slow or other dispute affecting the industry or a significant sector of it.

Some risks, such as regulatory and legislative risks, will apply to more than one of the categories above, for example to both the construction and operating phases of the project.

It is important to remember that the operational phase of the contract is by far the longest part of the contract. Hence, it is especially important that due consideration is given to the types of risk that might occur and the impact these may have in this phase. Furthermore, because it is not possible to identify all the risks that may occur over such a long period of time because there are too many unknowns, it is important that the contract includes a change control mechanism. This should be able to address both the changing requirements in a scheme and the changing nature of risks that may arise.

Assessment and quantification

Risk quantification is not an academic exercise. It is an important component of the value-for-money analysis. The private sector will charge a premium for assuming any risks which have been transferred to them by the public sector. This is reflected in the bid price for the project. This premium is only worth paying if it is less than the expected cost of the risk in question. Otherwise, it is more cost-effective for the public sector to retain the risk.

Risk quantification thus aims to estimate the net present cost of the risks which the public sector retains under the public sector comparator and the best PFI option. The difference between these two values is the net risk transfer from the public to the private sector.

The quality of the thinking which informs the risk analysis is just as important as the resulting output. The GIGO principle should be remembered in this regard – garbage in garbage out! Before attempting to quantify risks, it is, therefore, important to:

- consider whether the risk is inherently quantifiable. If it is not quantifiable, qualitative techniques should be used to assess the risk (low, medium, high based on informed judgements about likely probability and impact)
- consider the timing of the risk. Is it a one-off risk which is only likely to occur within the first year of the project or is it likely to span a longer period (conceivably the whole duration of the project)?
- consider how the risk might occur and with what impact on the project. Is it likely to impact on cost or time or both? Is it likely to have a low, medium or high impact on cost, time or both? Is it independent of other risks or is it likely to impact on other risks? Care should be taken to avoid double-counting
- consider the likelihood of the risk occurring. Does the risk have a low, medium or high probability of occurrence?

- consider whether historical data are available for quantifying the various risks. Sources of information to consider for NHS construction schemes include:
  - NHS Estates database of construction and development risks
  - organisation's own experience
  - organisation's technical advisers
  - experience of similar schemes, e.g. through results of post project evaluation
- consider what distribution curve should be used to represent each risk. Examples of some of the distributions which are commonly used in risk analysis are:
  - normal distribution – this groups the probability around the mean of the distribution. It is appropriate to use this when good information is available about the most likely value of a particular risk
  - S-curve – similar to the normal distribution but flatter
  - uniform distribution – this gives equal probability to all values between the minimum and maximum values
  - triangular distribution – this gives straight lines between the minimum and maximum and the mean of the distribution.

Techniques for quantifying risk

A risk analysis will typically consider the following for each risk which is quantifiable:

- financial impact of the risk if it were to occur
- the probability of the risk occurring
- the period over which the risk is likely to occur.

Techniques for valuing risks vary from informed rules of thumb to stochastic approaches involving Monte Carlo and Latin hypercube analyses.

Rules of thumb

Rules of thumb or heuristics are commonly used in decision making. For example, in considering an application for a mortgage, a financial institution may be prepared to lend the applicant up to three times his or her salary. Such decisions are often based on expert judgement, experience and other available information. In a similar manner, expert judgement and historical information may be used to determine what allowance to make for the various risks inherent in a project.

Given the rough and ready nature of these estimates, it is important for estimates derived on this basis to be supplemented with estimates derived from more objective and carefully reasoned approaches such as probability analyses. This is particularly important at the OBC stage and FBC stage when crucial decisions such as value for money and affordability need to be firmly and conclusively established.

Single-point and multi-point probability analysis

A single-point probability analysis, say for unforeseen ground conditions, could consist of an estimate of the cost of this risk occurring multiplied by its probability over the relevant time period.

In practice, more than one outcome is more likely. As an improvement on the single-point estimate, a number of individual estimates could be produced consisting of a most likely estimate, maximum estimate and minimum estimate. The respective probabilities for these three events may be multiplied to provide an expected value for this particular risk. For example, the expected value of ground conditions risk may be estimated as:

Possible cost p.a. (£m)	Probability	Allowance (£m)
1	0.25	0.25
3	0.6	1.8
7	0.15	1.05
Total		**3.1**

This example assumes the risk only applies in the first year of the project. The estimated value of the risk should be expressed in net present cost terms based on a 6% real discount rate. The evidence for the values (financial impact and probabilities) and all assumptions should be clearly stated.

Monte Carlo modelling

One way to ascertain what risk allowance is needed is to physically carry out the project. This is obviously not possible in practice. Models can, however, be developed to mimic the way the project is likely to perform in practice. The model is used to determine how the project reacts to different inputs. This can be considered as a form of statistical experiment.

In Monte Carlo simulation, a large number of hypothetical projects are generated to reflect the characteristics of the actual project. Each iteration is accomplished by replacing a risk variable with a random number drawn from the probability distribution selected to describe that variable, rather as a ball on a roulette wheel stops at random to select a winning number.

To implement the technique, at least three possible outcomes (lowest/optimistic, most likely and highest/pessimistic) should be defined for each risk variable, based on historical information and/or expert judgement. The computer uses a random number generator to choose values within the pre-defined range of values. Each time the project is simulated, independent sampling is made from the distributions defined for the risks. Some will show values towards the optimistic end of their ranges and others may show pessimistic values. The simulation uses the three point values and estimates all the possible outcomes between these values at random.

As a result of inputting data into the risk model in the form of a probability distribution, the results can be presented in the form of a statistical distribution. For example, a frequency distribution of all possible NPV outcomes would be produced for the whole project, instead of a single best guess estimate. Statistical methods may then be used to compute confidence intervals, the mean and variance of the distribution, the cumulative frequency curves and any other statistics of interest. The probability of different outcomes can be easily read off from the cumulative frequency curve.

It is recommended to perform 1000 iterations, each time sampling from the distribution which represents the particular risk. If too few iterations are performed, this will lead to clustering and unreliable results.

Latin hypercube

This is a recent development in sampling theory, designed to reproduce accurately the input distribution through sampling in fewer iterations compared with the Monte Carlo approach. The distinguishing feature of Latin hypercube sampling is stratification of the input probability distributions. A sample is then chosen from each stratified layer of the input distribution. Sampling is forced to represent values in each layer and is thus forced to recreate the input distribution. Convergence tests show that Latin hypercube sampling converges faster on the true distributions compared to Monte Carlo sampling.

Both methods are powerful aids to analysing risk. However, placed in the wrong hands, the techniques can be easily abused. Project sponsors will not generally have the skills in-house to use these techniques. It is also unlikely that sufficient and reliable data exist to determine the probability distributions. Such techniques should therefore be used with care. Robust and well-reasoned assumptions combined with simple techniques are more likely to generate meaningful results than sophisticated techniques applied to poor data.

Sensitivity analysis

Risk analysis may be supplemented with sensitivity analysis. Sensitivity analysis is the calculation of how changes in particular assumptions would affect net present values, total cost or other relevant project outcomes. Hence for any key assumptions which are made when assessing the values and probabilities of risks, sensitivity analysis may be used to test the robustness of those assumptions. It is particularly useful when the calculation of the NPVs for the project is not based on formal risk analysis. A comprehensive risk analysis gives the decision maker a good feel for the risks inherent in the project. Given the uncertainties in some of the assumptions underlying the risk analysis and the projected cash-flows, it is recommended that an estimate for risk transfer should be made under a best case scenario.

It is likely that the sensitivity analysis will concentrate on the assumptions made for the probabilities of different values of risk occurring. These assumptions are more likely to be less robust estimates than the estimates for the financial values of risks themselves.

It is recommended to extend the basic analysis to consider the 'switching value' or 'cross-over point'. This is the amount by which the variable(s) in question would have to change to reverse a decision. The likelihood of this outturn should also be assessed.

Project-specific discount rates: the Capital Asset Pricing Model

Capital is not a free good in the public sector. Public sector managers are required to manage capital resources efficiently and earn a 6% real return on capital employed. This Treasury-stipulated cost of capital figure has been in operation for a number of years now, notwithstanding changes in the rate of inflation and the cost of government borrowing.

A commonly used method to allow for risk is to vary the cost of capital figure or discount rate to reflect the risks inherent in the project. Projects with low systematic risks would be discounted at a lower rate than those with high systematic risks.

The Capital Asset Pricing Model (CAPM) provides a theoretical justification for the use of project-specific discount rates. It relates the return on a project directly to the risk involved for the shareholder and decomposes this into a risk-free rate of return (i.e. the return on gilts) and a risk-related return (i.e. risk premium). The risk premium in turn is made up of the 'average risk premium for the market' and the 'beta factor' of the particular company.

The CAPM distinguishes between *market* or *systematic* risks and *unique* or *unsystematic* risks. Market risks relate to economic trends which affect all investors equally and cannot be avoided or diversified by holding a portfolio of shares. In contrast, unsystematic risks are unique to a particular firm or sector. Examples of systematic risks are movements in inflation rates, interest rates, exchange rates, corporation tax rates and changes in government borrowing. Examples of unsystematic risks are the quality of the company's management team, poor employee–employer relations, under-investment in training, ineffectiveness of the company's research and development programme and other factors specific to the firm.

The beta factor is the correlation co-efficient between the returns on a market portfolio of investments and the returns on a particular investment. Stated alternatively, it is a measure of the sensitivity of the project to market movements. For example, if the beta value is greater than unity, this suggests the project is more sensitive to general market or systematic risks than the average project.

The CAPM is based on a number of restrictive assumptions, most notably:

- all investors maximise single-period expected utility of terminal wealth by choosing from different asset portfolios on the basis of the expected value and standard deviation of each asset
- all assets are perfectly divisible and marketable
- there are no taxes or transaction costs or bankruptcy costs
- the quantities of all assets are given
- all investors are price-takers
- all investors can borrow or lend unlimited amounts at the risk-free rate
- all investors have identical subjective estimates of the expected values, standard deviations and covariances of returns among all assets.

Symbolically, the CAPM may be represented as follows:

Cost of capital for project = $Rf + \beta(Rm\text{-}Rf)$ where
Rf   =   risk-free rate of return

Rm   =   average market return
β =   measure of systematic risk
(Rm-Rf) =   the market premium

If Rf = 6%, Rm = 11% and β = 0.9, the discount rate would be 6% + (0.95*5%) = 10.5%

Despite its intuitive appeal, the CAPM is difficult to implement in practice. Beta values are notoriously difficult to estimate and the results produced are often subject to huge statistical error. Beta values also change over time and are susceptible to changes in the debt-equity ratio (i.e. the level of gearing). Many companies are not quoted on the stock exchange with readily available security prices. This is certainly true of PFI special purpose vehicles. Returns on investment projects have been found to be related to a host of other factors other than systematic risks, e.g company size and dividend policy. Many of the underlying assumptions are unrealistic and, even if this is considered irrelevant, the model has not proved to produce much explanatory and predictive power. As a result of these limitations, other models have been developed to determine the cost of capital. The one which holds the most prospect is the Arbitrage Pricing Model (APM). Further details on the CAPM and APM are available in Arnold (1988) and Lumby (1995).

The main implication of this section is that manipulating the discount rate, whether subjectively determined or based on a rational model such as the CAPM, is not an effective method for dealing with risk. It is crude, arbitrary and simplistic. Personal attitude towards risk will influence the discount rate used. This will vary between project sponsors and other stakeholders, including shareholders. This method also implicitly assumes that risk increases over time, which may not be justified. Although the CAPM provides a more objective measure for determining the opportunity cost of capital, this approach is also fraught with difficulties.

Allocation principles

The way the risks are allocated will depend on the abilities of the parties involved in the transaction to manage the particular risks. The goal should be *optimum* transfer rather than *maximum* transfer. As noted previously, risk transfer will be one of the principal ways of achieving value for money. As a general rule, one would expect value for money to increase as risk is transferred to the private sector up to the optimum point. Once this point has been reached, any further risk transfer will result in a decline in value for money. The type of risk that needs to be transferred to achieve optimum value for money will depend on the nature of the particular project and the experience of the parties involved in the transaction. Although the public sector should have a clear position on which risks it is best placed to manage and hence retain, it should be prepared to negotiate with bidders to determine the exact allocation.

Box 4.3 provides examples of the sort of considerations which should inform the proposed allocation of the risks. If risks are not optimally allocated, this will either result in poor value for money to the public sector or create potential financial difficulties for the contractors and ultimately the success of the project. This lesson received prominence in the case study on procurement of custodial services at Bridgend and Fazakerley:

> The procurement of the custodial services . . . has produced some key learning points, not least . . . the need to identify potentially non-transferable risks as early as possible, for example the attempted transfer of occupancy risk proved wholly unacceptable as the private sector have no control over the way in which prisoners are allocated, or indeed the policy that dictates the number of prisoners. This can only be done in discussion with potential lenders, through or with financial advisers (HM Prison and Private Finance Panel 1996, p. 3).

Box 4.3: Risk transfer checklist

- Which party is best placed to control the events that may produce the risk?
- Who is best placed to manage the risk if it occurs?
- Whether the premium to be charged by the party assuming the risk is reasonable and cost-effective
- Whether the party holding the risk is able to sustain the consequences if the risk occurs
- Whether, as a result of transferring the risk, new risks are transferred back to the client

---

Figure 4.1 illustrates the close nexus between value for money and risk transfer. As PFI becomes better understood and experience accumulates over time, the properties of this curve are likely to alter.

Planning risks – risks surrounding obtaining planning permission are

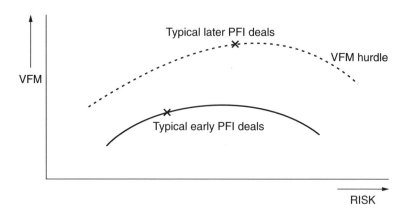

Figure 4.1: Risk transfer and value for money.

normally the responsibility of the procuring entity, while those relating to full planning permission and agreements under section 106 Town and Country Planning Act 1990 and section 278 Highways Act 1980 should generally be borne by the private sector.

Design risks – these are normally allocated to the private sector. This is particularly the case where the scheme adopts an innovative approach. If the design is not complete by financial close, this should not result in any change in price. The SPV should also be responsible for agreeing the design with other members of the consortium. This includes all aspects of the design and building works – structural integrity, foundations, air conditioning, etc.

This assumes the public sector has specified its requirements clearly and comprehensively in the form of an output specification, and that all relevant information about clinical adjacencies and interface between services has been made available to the SPV. If this is not the case, it will be difficult for the SPV to produce an appropriate design which does not require any variations.

The public sector client should reserve the right to introduce variations to the design of the facility at a reasonable cost during the construction and operational phases of the project. However, this right should only be exercised if considered strictly necessary as it will increase the cost of the project and reduce the SPV's control over the facility.

The costs associated with changes in design initiated by the procuring entity whether due to changes in its service requirements or 'external influences' should be borne by the client.

Construction and development risks – responsibility for ensuring that the services are delivered on time and within the agreed budget will normally rest with the private sector. The private sector will generally be responsible for complying with all relevant construction regulations such as construction, design and management (CDM) regulations. The main exceptions are when the time and/or cost over-runs result from events such as *'force majeure'* or 'relief' or 'compensation' (as previously described); unforeseen ground/site conditions under the footprint of existing buildings; a change in NHS-specific legislations/regulations; changes in the rate of VAT; and decanting from existing buildings.

The tariff and commencement date for the services will be specified in the contract. The contract will also give full details of the payment mechanism and the penalties to be incurred if the agreed quantity and quality of services are not delivered by the due date. The NHS should not normally be liable for any extra cost caused by time and cost overruns. The client should not pay any availability charge until the facilities are 'available' (i.e. commissioned and ready for occupation in accordance with the clauses of the project agreement). Failure to complete construction by the agreed date may not only lead to deferred payment, but a termination of the contract without the private sector having any recourse to compensation payments.

In some circumstances, the public sector may find it advantageous to accept completed facilities on a 'phased' basis. In such cases, the availability fee should be pro-rated accordingly. It is also possible for facilities to be completed ahead of schedule. Provision should be made in the contract for early notice to be given to the client in such cases as early completion may not necessarily be advantageous to the client.

Availability and performance risks – most of the risks under this category are normally assumed by the private sector either in whole or part. The main exception is when the risk results from changes (e.g. a change in specification during the operational phase) initiated by the procuring entity. Relief and *force majeure* events may impede or delay the performance of the contractor, and such risks should be shared.

The exact allocation of these risks will depend on how the contract is structured. For the private sector to take on the majority of availability and performance risks, it should be given responsibility for the delivery of the specified services and the maintenance of the building and associated facilities to agreed standards. In the NHS context, the main uncertainty relates to the private sector's ability to meet the required level of service provision, rather than the level of throughput in the building. The latter is outside their control.

In the NHS context, a facility is 'unavailable' if any of the following criteria are breached:

- environmental standards (heating, lighting and ventilation should be provided to the agreed standards)
- access (patients, staff and all lawful visitors should have unobstructed access to the hospital and its facilities)
- utility facilities (power, medical gases, water, sewerage facilities and communication systems should be provided to the agreed standards)
- building condition (the structural condition of the hospital should meet the agreed standard to enable the trust to occupy and use it for its intended purpose)
- health and safety condition (the physical condition of the hospital should satisfy NHS regulations and all other relevant legislations agreed in the contract)
- service provision (services should be provided to the agreed standards). For example, the agreed standard for catering services may be provision of food to patients within two hours of the scheduled time. A quality dimension should also be specified
- other breach in service delivery (failure other than those specified above which would prevent the designated areas from being used for their normal purpose).

If the procuring entity opts to use an area which has been declared unavailable, it should not pay the full availability fee for that area. The client should ensure continued use of the area does not inhibit the operator from undertaking any necessary remedies to restore full availability.

Operating cost risk – for the private sector to be exposed to operating cost risks, there should be no provision in the contract to pass fluctuations in operating costs onto the public sector client. A number of the risks in this category are likely to be shared, such as patient infection risks, risks surrounding the transfer of employment of staff to a new employer and general legislative/regulatory risks.

Variability of revenue – if payments to the private sector are genuinely variable and dependent upon availability of the services to the agreed standards and the volume of patient or treatment throughput, this is evidence that risk has been transferred. These risks are generally borne by the private sector. The main exceptions include variability of payments arising from changes in the amount of resources available for funding the service (e.g. healthcare provision), changes in the volume of demand for services (e.g. arising from demographic factors or medical technology) and changes in the epidemiology of the population in the catchment area.

Termination risks – difficulties often arise in long-term contracts which, if not properly managed, will cause the contract to unravel.

Risks in this category are usually allocated depending on which party causes the default event which leads to the termination.

Technology and obsolescence risks – medical advances and technology changes may require services to be delivered differently from the approach adopted at the start of the contract. For example, patients who are currently treated in hospitals may be treated in alternative settings. It would be inappropriate for the NHS to lock itself into paying for service provision which has become out of date and expensive.

The private sector should generally bear technology/asset obsolescence risks. The main exception is when a different solution has to be adopted because the procuring entity changes the output specification for the services it requires.

Control risks – ownership and control of the asset should rest with the private sector. This will allow the private sector to exert control over its operating costs and use the asset as it sees fit, subject to meeting the agreement with the procuring entity.

Residual value risk – this risk should be borne by the private sector. It refers to the potential variability between the actual residual value of the asset at the end of the contract and the expected value ascribed to it by the contractor at the outset. The residual value risk may be negligible or non-existent if the contract period covers all or most of the useful life of the asset, or if there are only limited alternative uses for the asset.

The procuring entity should avoid the risk of having to accept a potential liability at the end of the contract. There are a number of possibilities at the end of the contract, all of which should be considered when the scheme is being put together:

- re-tendering of the contract and transferring the asset to the new provider at a fair value for possible use in delivering the services which will be required
- the client may choose to purchase the underlying asset at market value
- the client may 'walk away' from the contract leaving the SPV to find another tenant or clear the site at their own expense.

The specific mechanisms used to effect risk transfer should be clearly demonstrated. One mechanism which is invariably used is the payment mechanism. The contract also has an important role to play (*see* next section). Box 4.4 shows how the payment mechanism may be structured to transfer risk to the operator. The example used is for an information technology project, but the basic principles are generic.

It is also good practice to summarise the agreed risk apportionment in the form of a risk allocation matrix. This should list the various risks

---

Box 4.4: Example of a payment mechanism for IS/IT projects

Availability payment – an element of payment for making the service available (e.g. the contract may specify that the system should be available at least 99% of the time between contract hours)

Performance payment – an element of payment for being able to meet specified performance targets, expressed in system response times, number of transactions processed or some other performance currency

Transaction/volume payment – payment linked to the volume of business processed or by the number of transactions

Incentive – linking payments to the overall performance of the business functions supported by the system or linking payments to usage. This approach will enable benefits to be shared between both parties

Source: cited in CIPFA (1997, p. 15)

---

and indicate whether they are borne wholly by the public sector, private sector or shared. By FBC stage, the exact proportions in which joint risks are shared should also be shown.

Contracts and risks

As previously discussed, the risks inherent in the project should be optimally allocated. Once allocated and agreed, it is important for this to be explicitly reflected in the relevant contract documentation. The fundamental purpose of the contract is to establish the rights, duties, obligations and responsibilities of the various parties as well as to allocate the relevant risks. Considerable care should be taken in drafting the contract clauses.

It is important for the party holding the risk to be equipped to deal with its probable financial implication. For example, it is unrealistic to impose liquidated damages of £50 000 per week on a two-man shuttering specialist contractor for liquidated and ascertained damages in the event of completion delays, even if it could be proved beyond reasonable doubt that they were responsible for delaying the project. The company would be unlikely to have the financial resources to absorb such costs. This example illustrates an important principle in risk allocation and management. The public sector client needs to ensure that whoever is bearing the risk has the resources, or access to the necessary resources, to absorb the risk in the event it were to materialise.

Surety bonds may be used to transfer risk to another party. A surety is a party who assumes liability for the debt, default or failure in duty of another party. The surety company may be an insurance company, a bank or a company specialising in sureties. A surety bond is different from an insurance policy: it guarantees the performance of a contractual duty while insurance protects a party from risk of loss. The bond may take the form of a bid bond (which ensures the contractor honours his tender bid), a performance bond (which ensures the project is completed in accordance with the terms of the contract in the event the contractor defaults), and a labour and material bond (which protects the client for labour and material used or supplied on the project).

Different types of contracts will exhibit a different allocation of risks. Figure 4.2 illustrates in simplified terms the broad allocation of risks which is expected under each form. PFI contracts are closer to the second and third types. Note the vast majority of the design and construction risks fall on the contractor.

It should be remembered that the operational phase of the contract is by far the longest part of the contract. Hence, it is important that due consideration is given to the types of risk that might occur and the impact these may have in this phase. Furthermore, because it is not possible to identify all the risks that may occur over such a long period of time, it is important that the contract includes a change control mechanism and other built-in flexibilities. This should be designed to address both the changing requirements in a scheme and the changing nature of risks that may arise.

This approach is now being actively promoted in local authorities to comply with the statutory requirements of the new Best Value regime. In recent guidance from the Department of the Environment, Transport and the Regions, *Preparing for Best Value* (April 1999), it advises that contracts lasting longer than five years should be inherently flexible to ensure the arrangements secure continuous improvement and can be adapted to address changing local and national priorities, as well as unforeseen circumstances.

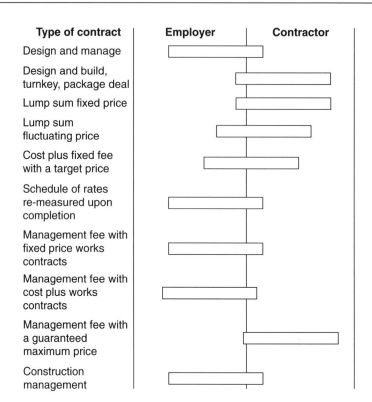

Figure 4.2: Risk by contract type
(adapted from Flanagan and Norman 1983).

Risk management strategy

Once risks have been identified, assessed and allocated, action needs to be taken to manage them. Attitudes to risk are important in risk management. Consider the following passage from WC Clark:

> Three young men could open either door they pleased. If they opened the one, there came out of it a hungry tiger, the fiercest and most cruel that could be procured, which would immediately tear them to pieces. But, if they opened the other door, there came forth a lady; the most suitable to her years and station that His Majesty could select from among his fair subjects. So I leave it to you, which door to open?
>
> The first man refused to take the chance. He lived safe and died chaste.
>
> The second man hired risk management consultants. He

collected all available data on lady and tiger populations. He brought in sophisticated technology to listen for growling and detect the faintest whiff of perfume. He completed checklists. He developed a utility function and assessed his risk attitude. Finally, sensing that in a few more years he would be in no condition to enjoy the lady anyway, he opened the optimal door. And was eaten by a low probability tiger.

The third man took a course in tiger training. He opened a door at random and was eaten by the lady (cited in Flanagan and Norman 1983, p. 67).

This quote illustrates some of the ways of coping with risk. The first man avoided the risk altogether by seeking alternative, less risky options (i.e. the do nothing option in this case). The second man sought additional information and expert opinion. Although he was ultimately eaten by the tiger, the event was delayed. The experience of the third man illustrates the need to analyse risk comprehensively. He died because his risk register only included the tiger instead of both the tiger and the lady.

A good risk management system should exhibit the following characteristics:

- all risks should be identified, classified and analysed before considering how they should be managed
- risk management needs to be continuous
- a suitable contingency plan should be developed to deal with the worst eventuality
- risk management should be integrated into the organisation's daily operations; it should not be complicated or burdensome
- it should also consider the resource (skills, etc.) requirements required to implement the risk management strategy.

In PFI contracts, the public sector should concentrate on managing those risks which it has retained. Its risk management strategy should detail how it plans to minimise these risks and what action will be taken if problems do occur. This should cover both risks which may directly arise from the project and risks associated with the realisation of benefits from the project. The risks (including control measures) should be monitored continuously.

For risks transferred to the private sector, it is not necessary for the public sector to see details of what risk management strategy the PFI partner is developing. However, the public sector client will want to have confidence that the PFI partner has a robust strategy for managing the risks they will bear. A firm indication should be given before a preferred bidder is selected of whether proposed financiers to the scheme are content with the proposed allocation and management of risks to be borne by the members of the consortium and the financiers themselves. The public sector should also satisfy itself that the contractor has the capability to absorb the financial consequences of the risks it will bear if these were to occur. This may take the form of parent company guarantees, cash reserves or access to credit. The performance of the contractor should be monitored over the life of the contract to ensure services are being delivered efficiently and effectively.

Risk and accounting treatment

In September 1997 the Treasury Task Force published interim guidance on how to account for PFI transactions. The Accounting Standards Board subsequently undertook work on how FRS5 should be interpreted in such transactions. This led to the publication of *Amendment to FRS5: Note F*, in September 1998. At the time of writing, HM Treasury is still in the process of translating the principles in 'Note F' in guidance which will apply to the whole public sector.

In line with earlier guidance, risk continues to have a direct bearing on the accounting treatment of the transaction (*see*, especially, Treasury Task Force's *How to Account for PFI Transactions*, September 1997). The following risks are particularly material to this assessment:

- performance risks
- pricing risks
- operating cost risks
- design risks
- demand risks
- residual value risks.

The financial impact of the relevant risks should be assessed and modelled under a range of scenarios from best case to worst case. In addition, the assessment of whether the transaction should be capitalised on the private sector's balance sheet (i.e. an operating lease as opposed to a finance lease) should be underpinned by considerations about the amount of risk capital (equity) in the project. Genuine commercial risk will be demonstrated where there is a significant amount of equity capital involved and the equity holders are exposed to the potential for significant variability in their expected return and there is some risk that their actual return may fall below the lenders' return.

As discussed in Chapter 6, the full business case should provide an assessment of the accounting treatment of the scheme. This should be underpinned by professional advice from the procuring entity's external auditors or a reputable accounting firm. This assessment should be based on all relevant aspects of the transaction and should be fully consistent with all documentation on the project, particularly the contract.

Conclusion

This chapter concludes with a list of good practice tips on conducting a risk analysis:

- project sponsors should consider risks from the outset of the project
- make sure risks have been comprehensively identified and assessed
- involve all relevant stakeholders in risk audit meetings and brainstorming workshops to ensure robust identification and understanding of the risks surrounding the project
- risk analysis is an iterative process, not a one-off activity
- adopt a prudent and evidence-based approach to risk quantification: remember the garbage in garbage out principle
- approach risk analysis as a commercial activity rather than as an academic exercise
- avoid inappropriate and suboptimal allocation of risks: value for money and the project economics will be undermined
- ensure all risks allocated to the project company are written explicitly and unambiguously into the contract
- avoid surprises: make sure you have developed a robust risk management strategy
- risk analysis pervades the whole project and has direct implications for scoping the deal, value for money, affordability, bankability, contract and payment mechanism, accounting treatment, and project viability and management during the operational period
- remember that this part of the deal and the business case will attract close scrutiny from the approvers and external watchdog bodies such as the NAO.

CHAPTER FIVE

The assessment of value for money

As noted before, there are two fundamental criteria for judging the efficacy of PFI projects: (i) value for money must be unambiguously demonstrated for any expenditure by the public sector and (ii) the private sector must genuinely assume risks which it is best placed to manage. For services sold to the public sector, our classical PFI model, these two requirements are inextricably linked. Failure to meet the value-for-money (including risk transfer) requirement will, in all probability, render the project unapprovable. The public expenditure context for capital investments has now changed. It is no longer a choice between PFI and nothing; exchequer funded (in whole or part) alternatives are now feasible.

This chapter discusses the issues involved in assessing and demonstrating value for money. It is written largely from an economic (business case) perspective. It provides a number of practical tools and tips for negotiating more effective PFI deals and aiding the preparation of fit-for-purpose business cases. Although the procurement is assumed to be a healthcare facility, the principles apply equally to other types of procurement.

Three value-for-money decisions

Best value for money is the optimum combination of whole-life costs, benefits and risks. There are three crucial value-for-money decisions to be made in capital investment projects: (i) decide whether to proceed with the project at all and, if so, identify the best service solution, (ii) whether to proceed using PFI or a conventional procurement route and (iii) what supplier to select to meet the service requirement. These decisions are made at different stages in the procurement process. The first decision is made at the SOC/OBC stage. The work done at the OBC stage allows a preliminary view to be taken on the second decision. However, in most cases, this can only be reliably made following a competitive tendering process. The third decision must, by definition, be informed by the procurement process.

All three decisions are important. They need to be underpinned by firm evidence and analyses. The first and second tests should be based on a rigorous economic appraisal, based on the conventions outlined in HM Treasury's 'Green Book' (*Economic Appraisal in Central Government*, HM Treasury 1991, 1997) and NHSE's *Capital Investment Manual* (1999).

As noted previously, risk transfer will be one of the principal ways of achieving value for money. As a general rule, one would expect value for money to increase as risk is transferred to the private sector up to the optimum point. Once this point has been reached, any further risk transfer will result in a decline in value for money. The type of risk that needs to be transferred to achieve optimum value for money will depend on the nature of the particular project and the experience of the parties involved in the transaction. Although the public sector should have a clear position on which risks it is best placed to manage and hence retain, it should be prepared to negotiate with bidders to determine the exact allocation. It cannot be overemphasised that the goal is *optimum* transfer, not *maximum* transfer (*see* Figure 4.1).

Value-for-money test 1: the OBC stage

This section describes the process involved in satisfying the first value-for-money test. For presentational ease, the SOC stage is omitted from the discussion. This is principally because the analyses undertaken at the SOC stage are not designed to test value for money in any rigorous way. The SOC is designed to identify the health service need for any proposed scheme. There is no expectation for the SOC process to result in a preferred option, only a set of shortlisted options which are relevant to the health service needs and are affordable to commissioners of the trust's services. Moreover, it is expected that the OBC should refine, update and extend the work conducted at the SOC stage to ensure that any proposed scheme is founded on a firm analytical base.

The OBC is thus a crucial stage. The work undertaken as part of the OBC enables the project to be properly scoped and costed. The OBC also serves the vital role of a public sector comparator for gauging PFI bids for value for money. PSCs are discussed later in this chapter.

Once a clear business need has been identified for the project, it is important that all feasible options for meeting the expressed need are explored. HM Treasury (1997) sets out the process and technical conventions which public sector departments should follow in undertaking economic appraisals. These are further reinforced in the Department of Health's *Capital Investment Manual* (CIM). A revised edition of the CIM will be issued later this year (NHSE 1999).

The main steps are:

- step 1 – define the strategic context
- step 2 – specify objectives of the project and benefit criteria
- step 3 – generate options
- step 4 – identify and measure the benefits
- step 5 – identify and quantify the costs
- step 6 – identify the preferred option
- step 7 – test assumptions and validate the preferred option
- step 8 – present the OBC.

Strategic context

The starting point for an option appraisal should be a clear definition of the strategic context. This should be informed by Ministerial objectives for the NHS and the local HImP. This should address issues such as the current and future health service needs of the population (taking into account all determinants of healthcare provision, including demographic changes, medical and technological advances, changes in patients' expectations, etc.); activity projections for all types of in-patient, day case and out-patient activities; performance targets (length of stay, bed occupancy rates, day case rates, etc.); the service deficiencies to be remedied; the changes required in the quantity or quality of service to be provided; possible changes in the geographical distribution of services and the health needs of the various segments of the population; resourcing issues (including affordability); alternative models for delivering services or working with other healthcare providers to develop alternatives to hospital care; and the condition and utilisation of the estate relative to current and future service needs.

The main output from this phase is a clear vision of future services and levels of service; documentation of the trust's capital investment strategy and clear service objectives; demonstration of an understanding of the local health economy and the trust's position within it;

demonstration of the strategic risks facing the organisation and its ability to deliver healthcare to the required standard and quantity; a preliminary indication of the affordability envelope within which any proposed investment must be contained; and possible models for reconfiguring services.

Before proceeding to the next stage, it is important for service planners to revisit and challenge the assumptions underlying the work undertaken to define the strategic context. Rationalisation of services cannot be achieved overnight. They can also be costly. Once implementation commences, it is difficult to reverse such plans if they are found to be out of line with new national trends or priorities.

Objectives and benefit criteria

Having set the strategic direction for change, objectives must be specified to meet the stated service requirements. These objectives provide the basis for formulating options for appraisal, developing the benefit criteria against which options (service models and site options) may be assessed, and providing criteria for judging the success of the investment.

Project objectives should be consistent with wider government objectives such as those articulated in *The New NHS: modern, dependable* (Department of Health 1997), *Our Healthier Nation* (Department of Health 1998) and *A First Class Service: quality in the NHS* (Department of Health 1998). Objectives should have 'SMART' attributes (specific, measurable, achievable, relevant and time-constrained). An example of a SMART objective is to reduce facility running costs by 10% within five years. It is good practice to rank objectives in priority order. This will help with the evaluation of options and, if necessary, the tailoring of options to match available resources.

Benefit criteria should be derived from the objectives. These typically fall into three categories: benefits which can be quantified financially; benefits which can be quantified, but not in financial terms; and benefits which cannot be easily quantified.

Examples of benefit criteria for capital schemes are:

- quality of clinical care
- patient accessibility
- quality of accommodation
- future flexibility
- accessibility to staff
- impact on teaching, education and training.

Generating options

Once a set of objectives has been specified, the next task is to generate a set of options for meeting the objectives. This process should not be unduly constrained. There is a common tendency for one particular (preconceived) option to be allowed to dominate considerations and constrain the choice of options. It is therefore important to consider all the available options. These should include capital and non-capital options, as well as a do nothing and/or do minimum option.

This stage should be viewed as an opportunity to consult all stakeholders, particularly commissioners of the organisation's services, about possible solutions for meeting the objectives. It is recognised that it will not be possible to analyse each option in detail. A credible shortlist should be drawn up for detailed analysis. The selection of the shortlist is an important matter of judgement. It is important to record the justification for eliminating options at this stage. Possible reasons may include physical, statutory and financial constraints. For example, it may not be feasible to erect a building of an appropriate size, shape and form on a given site. Options which violate objective constraints may be eliminated, e.g. funding constraints.

It is important to retain the 'do nothing' or 'do minimum' option as a 'baseline'. This may not be a viable option. However, it will serve to highlight the disadvantages of maintaining the *status quo*, for example exorbitant maintenance costs associated with the use of substandard accommodation. It will rarely be necessary to select more than six options for detailed appraisal.

Shortlisted options should be specified clearly to facilitate evaluation of their costs, benefits and risks. This should cover factors such as:

- intended service outcomes
- expected workloads and throughput (in-patients, day cases, etc.)
- functional content (beds by speciality, support services, etc.)
- accessibility for patients, staff and visitors
- staffing consequences
- implications for the estate (including land sales)
- effects on other services
- flexibility to accommodate changes in policy
- expected impact on performance indicators
- impact on financial performance.

Measure the benefits (both financial and non-financial)

This step involves identification, quantification, valuation (where feasible) and presentation of the benefits associated with shortlisted options. It will often be difficult to measure expected benefits in monetary terms. The ultimate value of a capital development will be an improvement in the health of the population served by that facility. What is more observable is a series of 'intermediate outputs', such as number of cases treated, number of in-patient days, improved access to services, better quality of care, etc. To demonstrate the differences in benefits between options, it is helpful to describe clearly the service provided by each option and how this represents an improvement over existing provision. This should be followed by a more explicit assessment of service benefits.

Benefits which can be quantified financially (e.g. cost savings) should be included in the cost analysis of options (*see* next step below). Non-financial benefits should be assessed by means of weighting and scoring approaches. This would attach weights to the various benefit criteria to reflect their relative importance so that the total weights amount to 100. For each option the criteria are weighted then scored between 0 and 10. The weight should be multiplied by the score to produce a weighted score for each criterion and then aggregated to produce a total weighted score for each option. Ignoring cost and risks from the equation for the time being, the higher the total weighted score the more attractive is the particular option.

Some options will generate benefits earlier than others. The valuation should also take this into account. For example, timing of benefits could be used as one of the benefit criteria. The process and reasoning behind the scores and weights must be clearly recorded. It is the number of people involved in the process and their expertise which lends credibility to this method of assessment. It is, therefore, important to involve the right people and conduct the process fairly.

Identify and quantify the costs

This step aims to identify and assess the total cost of implementing each option over its relevant time horizon. The appraisal period should normally equate to the intended period of use of the asset. For PFI options, the length of the contract period should also be used as well as the life span of the asset. New hospitals are assumed to have a life span of 60 years. Information services and technology projects are conventionally appraised over eight years.

In costing each capital option, estimates should be made of:

- capital costs
- operating costs
- opportunity costs of resources already owned
- consequential costs borne by others.

It is worth unpacking capital costs as it involves a number of significant cost elements:

- *land*: the purchase price of new land or opportunity cost of existing land
- *works or building costs*: these will usually be refurbishment and upgrading or construction of a new building, or a combination of both. They also include *on-costs*. On-costs are the additional capital costs which arise from the interaction of individual departments within a development and the relationship of that development to the particular site and existing buildings. They include communications (e.g. corridors, lifts, stairs, etc.), external works (e.g. roads, paths, drainage, etc.), auxiliary buildings (e.g. bin stores, bicycle sheds, meter housings, etc.) and abnormal (i.e. exceptional factors which increase capital costs on either the building or the engineering services such as demolitions, adverse soil conditions and alterations to existing buildings)
- *professional fees*: these include fees for architects, quantity surveyors, engineers, lawyers, surveyors, site supervisors, commissioning officers, project managers and other professionals as required
- *equipment*: this will include new equipment, installation costs and the value of transferred equipment. Equipment within healthcare facilities is typically grouped into four categories depending on their specialist nature and space implications.

Planning contingency: this is an allowance to cover risks up to construction of the facility. It does not obviate the need for a full risk analysis since it does not cover risks during the post-construction phase. Care should, however, be taken to avoid double-counting.

Revenue costs are also a major category. These include staff costs, management and administrative costs, consumables and equipment maintenance, estate costs (building maintenance, grounds maintenance, local authority business rates, utilities, estate management, etc.) and services such as catering, laundry and housekeeping.

Identify preferred option

Capital charges, VAT and all non-resource costs should be stripped out of the costs before evaluating the total net present cost of each short-listed option. All cashflows should be expressed in real terms or constant prices (i.e. at a specified price level which excludes inflation). Inflation should be excluded except where the cost of some inputs exceed normal inflation, in which case only the element above normal inflation should be included. The net present value method is the recommended method for evaluating the options. This method makes it possible to compare options with different time horizons and a different profile of capital and revenue cashflows on a consistent basis. This is done by converting all future cashflows associated with each option to their equivalent value today (i.e. their present value). The standard test discount rate is 6%. Note that this is a real discount rate and should only be applied to cashflows which are also expressed in real terms. Other rates may be appropriate (subject to clearance from HM Treasury) where:

- time preference for income or public expenditure is not relevant to the project in question
- the cashflows are nominal
- there is *exceptional* systematic risk
- there is specific policy adjustment for the particular public sector department
- discounting extends to the very long term (beyond 50 years).

Issues relating to the costs of capital and discounting are discussed in greater detail in HM Treasury (1997).

With the NPV method, the preferred option is the one with the highest positive net present value (i.e highest ratio of benefits over costs). This approach assumes all costs and benefits can be valued. If, as is more usual with health schemes, it is not feasible to value all costs and benefits, the preferred option would be the one with the lowest net present cost (assuming the options appraised deliver the same outputs). In selecting the preferred option, account should be taken of the results of the weighting and scoring analysis for non-financial costs and benefits. The results of the risk analysis should also be taken into account.

Test assumptions and validate the preferred option

The assumptions underlying the cashflows for each option should be tested by undertaking sensitivity analysis on variables with uncertain values. If the ranking of the options does not change when different assumptions are made, then the preferred option is likely to be robust. If the conclusion changes with variations in the underlying assumptions, the likelihood of the change in the assumptions should also be assessed. If this outcome is not likely, then the choice of the preferred option may remain robust. Otherwise, the choice is unduly risky. If none of the feasible options is robust, less risky options should be developed.

It is recommended that sensitivity tests should be undertaken on all variables with uncertain values and assumptions which are not evidence-based. Typical variables for testing may include: capital costs, revenue costs, delays in availability of public funds, length of the construction period, assumptions about savings, income due to trust, changes in commissioning or NHS trust strategy which may affect assumptions about activity levels (hence size of the facility), changes in the functional content of the facility, weights and scores used to assess non-financial benefits, and assumptions underlying the risk estimate. It is not sufficient to make arbitrary variations in the underlying parameters, say 10%, around cost or benefit. The probability of the likely range of variation should be assessed, based on past experience and/or expert knowledge.

Affordability

Once the best value-for-money option has been selected, it is important to assess its affordability. The best option must satisfy both the value for money and affordability tests. To state the obvious, an option may represent best value for money but may not be affordable. The converse is also true. It is, therefore, important to assess the year-on-year impact of the preferred option on prices to commissioners and the trust's income and expenditure position.

The affordability analysis should take into account the following (as appropriate):

- the revenue cost of existing services
- changes in revenue costs resulting from changes in services provided
- capital costs and the resultant implications for capital charges

- equipment and information technology costs
- whole-life costs
- the cost of risks associated with the project
- project costs (e.g. fees and decant costs)
- proceeds from any land sales
- VAT which cannot be recovered
- the impact of any price inflation on costs in excess of the assumed rate of general inflation.

Like the economic appraisal, it is also prudent to test the assumptions underlying the affordability/financial analysis. If the affordability test is breached, the trust and its commissioners should consider opportunities for reducing costs. This includes options such as phasing the preferred option differently, reducing the size of the preferred option, adopting a different design, and altering the mix of new build and refurbishment.

Value-for-money test 2: the bidding stage

HM Treasury (1995) makes clear 'Competition is the best guarantor of value for money. As a result of the competitive process, the best PFI options should emerge' (p. 19). The process for undertaking a competitive exercise was described in Chapter 3. Effective competition squeezes out inefficiency and monopoly profit. Competition should be maintained for as long as possible. At the same time, the procurer should be mindful of the costs which are associated with a long and protracted procurement process. A fine judgement should be made, therefore, about the point at which the preferred bidder is chosen.

Two key points are worth reiterating: (i) the need for the competition to be fair and full and (ii) the need for the public sector client to prepare properly before commencing the procurement.

The EC procurement rules are designed to satisfy the first point. It is therefore important for the spirit and letter of these rules to be followed. The second point underlines the need to research the market, understand all aspects of the project and the procurement process, and ensure the relevant skills are in place to conduct meaningful and hard negotiations.

Although a properly conducted PFI process will help the public sector to choose the best PFI bid, this bid will not necessarily produce the best value for money. In principle, it may be possible for the public sector to outperform the private sector on value-for-money grounds. It is for this reason that public sector comparators are particularly important. This is discussed below in the section on the third value-for-money test.

Where it is not realistic to develop a PSC or competition has been very limited, alternative benchmarks should be used. There may sometimes be additional benchmarks available. For example, in the case of accommodation projects, the rent of similar standard accommodation; and for telecommunications services, charges for using public networks.

The value-for-money test at this stage is not limited to the procurement of the services in the OBS. It also applies to the process by which advisers have been selected, funding solution determined (e.g. bond versus conventional project finance) and financiers appointed, and the basis on which surplus assets (e.g. land) have been incorporated in the deal. These are all part of the value-for-money equation at this stage. Again, competition has a major role to play in these crucial decisions. In the absence of fierce competition, credible benchmarking evidence may serve as a proxy for value for money.

Not only do these decisions need to be made optimally, they also need to be implemented cost-effectively. For example, obtaining best value for money from the appointment of advisers defeats the objective if they are not used and managed effectively.

Value-for-money test 3: the FBC stage

At the FBC stage, the key value-for-money decision is to choose the best *method of funding* the preferred service solution identified at the OBC stage. The options include using exchequer finance, private finance or some combination of the two. This will typically require comparing the best PFI bid with the public sector comparator. This judgement must be based on the results of four key analyses: (i) economic appraisal (based on an updated PSC); (ii) formal risk analysis; (iii) assessment of non-financial costs and benefits; (iv) sensitivity analysis.

Public sector comparator

As noted earlier, the preferred option identified at the OBC stage has an important role to play in gauging value for money following the competitive tendering process. The preferred option identified at the OBC stage provides the basis for the PSC. This may be defined as a risk-adjusted estimate of how much it would cost the public sector (as a traditional supplier) to provide the facility and associated services defined in the output specification for the project.

The practice of applying and constructing PSCs varies between departments. PSCs are routinely used in the NHS as they are seen as an example of good practice. Figure 5.1 illustrates the Treasury's views on the circumstances under which PSCs are required.

To allow a like-for-like comparison with PFI bids, it is important to ensure that the PSC is calculated on a basis consistent with that used to assess PFI bids. In particular, it should be tailored to the same output specification as the PFI bids, both quantity and quality of services. This does not mean that the public sector should emulate the private sector's solution. However, the public sector should not attempt to manipulate the outcome of this value-for-money test by deliberately producing ineffective and inefficient solutions which will not satisfy the requirements of the output specification or which do not reflect recent construction practices in the public sector.

It should not be assumed that there would be long delays in availability of public capital. This would skew the outcome in favour of the PFI option as the effect of this assumption is to enable the PFI option to deliver benefits earlier than the PSC, benefits which result from a spurious assumption rather than from private sector innovation. Instead, the base estimate should be provided on the assumption that public funds will be available over the same timescale as the best PFI option. Sensitivity analysis should be conducted to explore the effects of any evidence-based uncertainty about the timing in the availability of public funds for the development. Advice should be sought from the relevant Regional Office about the likely duration of any delay in funding via the conventional route.

The PSC should also be risk-adjusted since private sector quotes for a PFI project will include a premium for carrying the risks transferred by the public sector. An assessment should be made of the likely costs of risks retained by the public sector under the PSC. This should encompass the risks of developing and constructing the facility and then operating it to provide a service which meets the performance standards specified in the output specification over the life of the project. Prior to the introduction of PFI, this type of analysis was unfamiliar to much of the public sector. The PSC is, of course, much more than simply a capital option. It should also cover the whole-life running costs of the facility.

In most cases, once the OBC has been approved, it should not

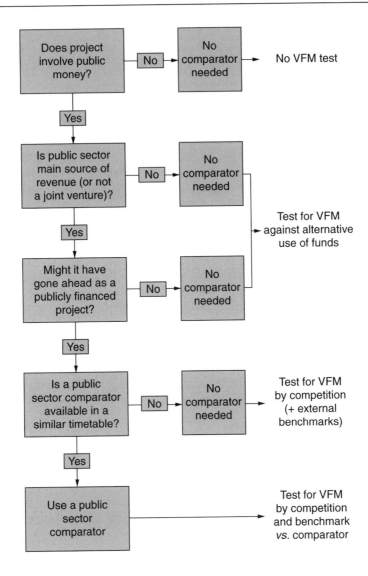

Figure 5.1: Public sector comparators (adapted from Private Finance Panel November 1995).

normally be necessary to do any further work on the PSC, except to uplift it for differential inflation. However, the key assumptions which underlie the OBC should be kept under review. The PSC should be revised to reflect any material changes in the assumptions. It may also be necessary to revise the PSC as bids are received from the private sector. NHS trusts should not emulate any innovative ideas from the private sector or any aspect of the private sector's solution. Where bids are made which envisage a wider scope than the NHS trust originally envisaged, it is legitimate to enhance the PSC to match the scope of the bids. All refinements should be motivated by the need to ensure the PSC provides a fair value-for-money benchmark.

The Treasury Task Force encourages procurers to disclose the PSC to bidders, especially where competition is strong. This provides valuable information to bidders about procurers' requirements and the affordability ceiling for the project, and engenders confidence that the public sector has thought through the project properly. If competition is limited, however, disclosure of the PSC may weaken the public sector's bargaining position. 'Each case should be judged on its merits but to ensure proper stewardship of public assets, the public sector should never disclose information that weakens its negotiating position' (Treasury Task Force 1998 No. 2, p. 17).

To enable the adequacy of the PSC to be judged, it is important to state the following information explicitly and pull it together in an appropriate section of the business case:

- description of the design solution of the PSC and how it differs from the PFI solution
- construction period of the PSC compared to the construction period of the PFI solution with an explanation of any difference
- comparison of the functional content of both options including number and type of beds, physical size (measured in square metres) and amount of new build and refurbishment
- enumeration of the build-up of the capital cost of both options (including the treatment of building cost inflation under the PSC as measured by the Median Index of Public Sector Building Tender Prices, MIPS)
- a description of the risks retained by the public sector under both the PSC and PFI solution
- a statement of all assumptions underlying the cashflows associated with both options.

Like the risk analysis, this part of the business case will attract close and detailed scrutiny from the approvers. This will also be of particular interest to external bodies like the National Audit Office. In circumstances where the PSC is adjudged to be flawed, the procuring entity may be required to develop a 'conventionally funded option' (CFO). The CFO attempts to generate a like-for-like comparison by estimating the cost to the exchequer of implementing an identical solution to the one proposed by the private sector. This is based on the private sector's design, similar functional content, bed complement and timescale for start on site.

Making the value-for-money comparison

Assuming the PSC has been updated and robustly constructed to facilitate a fair comparison, the value-for-money assessment should be straightforward. The aim is to assess the relative costs, benefits and risks of the PSC and the best PFI bid to determine the optimum funding method. This assessment should follow the technical conventions laid down in HM Treasury's 'Green Book' (*Economic Appraisal in Central Government*, HM Treasury 1991, 1997) and NHSE's *Capital Investment Manual* (1999). The main steps for assessing the options are outlined above in the section which deals with the first value-for-money test.

The value-for-money decision should be informed by the results of four crucial analyses:

- The discounted cash flows/economic appraisal – this estimates the net present cost and equivalent annual cost of the cashflows associated with the two options, taking account of actual cashflows and excluding all non-cash transfers such as capital charges and VAT. The PFI option must be appraised over both the primary contract period (typically 30 years) and the life of the asset (typically 60 years for new hospital buildings). The PSC should only be appraised over the life span of the asset as it is assumed the public sector would not walk away from the asset before it has reached the end of its useful life. Equivalent annual costs should be calculated by dividing the NPVs by the relevant cumulative discount factor to reflect differences in the life spans of the options.
- Quantified risk analysis – this evaluates the value of the risk retained by the public sector under both options. In general, the public sector will retain considerably less risk under the PFI option compared to the PSC. This reflects the goal of optimum risk transfer from the public to the private sector, admittedly at a premium. This is one of the main reasons why the net present cost/equivalent annual cost (NPC/EAC) of the PFI option (before risk adjustment) is usually greater than the NPC/EAC of the PSC.
- The assessment of non-financial costs and benefits – this evaluates the relative differences between the two options in delivering net benefits which cannot be valued in monetary terms and reflected in the discounted cash flow analysis. These differences may result from the design solution and management arrangements adopted under both options. They are usually assessed by weighting and scoring techniques.

- The sensitivity analysis – this is designed to test the assumptions and any uncertainties present in the three analyses described above. If properly conducted, it will demonstrate that the preferred option has been robustly developed and insensitive to changing assumptions.

All four sets of analyses must be technically sound and driven by evidence-based or carefully reasoned assumptions if the decision is to be well-founded. It is, therefore, important to record explicitly the methodology, data sources and evidential basis of all assumptions which underlie these analyses. It is also helpful to briefly describe the process adopted and the professional status of those who conducted the work or helped to implement it.

Summary outputs (based on a hypothetical example) from these analyses are shown below in Table 5.1. In this case, the results conclusively demonstrate the value-for-money superiority of the PFI option.

Results of sensitivity tests should also be provided. Table 5.2 provides an indicative example. Other sensitivities should be conducted, as appropriate, such as effect of variations in financing costs/interest

Table 5.1(a): NPC and EAC calculations

NPC/EAC	30 years (PFI)	60 years (PFI)	60 years (PSC)
NPC of total estimated costs (£m)	650	725	715
NPC of project risks retained by the public sector (£m)	0.30	0.5	20
Total risk-adjusted NPC (£m)	650.30	725.5	735
EAC of total estimated costs (£m)	44.55	42.5	41.9
EAC of risk retained (£m)	0.02	0.03	1.17
Total risk-adjusted EAC (£m)	44.57	42.53	43.07

(b) Total weighted score for PSC and PFI options

Attribute	PFI	PSC	Comments
Quality of clinical care	25	25	
Accessibility to staff and visitors	15	15	
Patient accessibility	10	10	
Quality of accommodation	30	20	
Future flexibility	25	20	
Impact on teaching, education and training	20	20	
Total weighted score	125	110	

Table 5.2: Sensitivity results

60 years sensitivity	PFI (£m)	PSC (£m)	Difference (£m)
NPC of base cashflows (risk-adjusted)	725.5	735	9.5
Activity changes and impact on projected savings			
10% increase in FCEs			
10% decrease in FCEs			
20% decrease in FCEs			
Capital expenditure			
10% increase in capital expenditure			
20% increase in capital expenditure			
10% decrease in capital expenditure			
Operating costs			
10% increase in operating costs			
20% increase in operating costs			
10% decrease in operating costs			

rates, inflation, income from any revenue generating scheme and land proceeds.

Affordability

As noted previously, the affordability of the preferred option should also be assessed. The preferred option should satisfy both the value-for-money and affordability tests. It is possible for an option to satisfy the three value-for-money tests discussed earlier without being affordable. One reason for this is the inclusion of additional non-resource costs such as VAT and capital charges in the affordability analysis. These costs are excluded from the economic appraisal.

Sensitivity analysis should be conducted on the key parameters underlying the affordability analysis. The following variables have been found to be particularly significant in considerations of affordability: changes in capital cost, revenue cost, interest rates, inflation estimate or proposed index for uplifting payments to the project company, availability of public funding (applies to PSC only), capital charges estimates, change in purchasing strategy (hence activity estimates) and delays in receipt of savings.

Presentationally, the summary results of the affordability analysis may appear as shown in Table 5.3. This is a hypothetical example to

Table 5.3: Affordability analysis

Cost category	PSC (£000)	PFI (£000)	Difference/ saving (£000)
Staff-related costs	4000	3700	−300
Non-staff costs	200	180	−20
Service charges	290	400	+110
Capital charge (depreciation and interest)/facility charge	750	670	−80
Other costs	180	200	+20
Total costs (equipment replacement, rates, energy, utilities, maintenance)	5420	5150	270
Total income	5220	5600	−380
Deficit/surplus (+/−)	+200	−450	−250

illustrate the basic principles of the affordability analysis. Note, a minus sign denotes a saving or surplus. The example shows that the PSC is not affordable. It results in an affordability gap of £200 000. In contrast, the PFI option is affordable and releases an extra £250 000 in savings to commissioners.

Managing affordability gaps

If the affordability analysis reveals the preferred value-for-money option is not affordable, there are a number of options for eliminating the funding gap. Options to consider include one or more of the following:

- find additional sources of funds (e.g. from surplus land if available, revenue support from the commissioners of services, savings from elsewhere within the NHS, revenue support from the Regional Office, third party revenue, etc.)
- negotiate more competitive or flexible prices from the project company (e.g. smoother profiling of the payments over the life of the contract)
- work with the project company to find a more cost-effective solution or identify other sources of efficiencies (e.g. consider possibilities for generating income from third parties or selling services as appropriate)
- consider more flexible and cost-effective funding solutions

- alter the scope of the preferred option (e.g. alter the functional content or the quality or quantity of the services offered)
- consider other solutions (e.g. phasing in services over different time-scales, altering the mix of refurbishment and new-build, etc).

A letter of support from the main commissioner(s) should always be submitted with the business case to confirm the commissioners are willing and able to meet the costs of the scheme and unequivocally support the service model and all underlying planning assumptions. Their views on the wider impact of the scheme and activity and performance assumptions are particularly important.

Conclusion

This chapter concludes with a list of good practice tips on conducting an economic appraisal and affordability analysis:

- make sure the project is set within a clear strategic context and is driven by service priorities
- objectives should be clearly defined. 'SMART' objectives make the task of option appraisal and *ex post* evaluation easier
- all objectives underlying the option appraisal should be stated explicitly
- objectives which are not evidence-based and/or characterised by uncertainty should be tested
- clear and relevant benefit criteria should be developed to assess the options
- the basis on which options have been shortlisted should be stated explicitly
- the costs, benefits and risks associated with the shortlisted options should be rigorously assessed
- the option appraisal should conform to the technical conventions (discount rate, appraisal horizon, etc.) outlined in HM Treasury's 'Green Book'
- the preferred option should be consistent with the results of the option appraisal and should be justified on grounds of value for money and affordability
- the preferred option should be robust to plausible changes in the key underlying assumptions and variables. It should be underpinned by comprehensive sensitivity analysis

- all three value-for-money decisions should be satisfied at the FBC stage
- PSCs, risk analysis and all other aspects of the economic appraisal must be technically sound
- unequivocal evidence should be provided to demonstrate affordability and ability to meet the cost implications of the preferred option
- clear evidence should be provided to show how any affordability gap will be absorbed.

CHAPTER SIX

Preparing and presenting the Full Business Case

This chapter summarises the purpose of the FBC, the key approval criteria and the main issues to address in the FBC. It concludes with a list of pitfalls to avoid to reduce the risk of not obtaining approval for the project. If the project has been executed properly throughout the various phases, the risk of not obtaining approval at the FBC stage should be negligible or non-existent.

The contents of the FBC should be dictated by the requirements of those who are involved in the approval process. For schemes above the project sponsors' delegated limits, this will typically include NHSE's Regional Office, NHSE Headquarters, HM Treasury, and both Treasury and Health Ministers.

External stakeholders such as the National Audit Office, trade unions and the public at large will also have an interest in the FBC, particularly in whether the preferred option meets the value-for-money test and other approval criteria. In line with the government's policy on 'openness', business cases are now public documents. Considerable care needs to be taken to strike the right balance between commercially sensitive material and what is required to satisfy the approval requirement.

Although based on the experience of the health sector, much of the material in this chapter (including the process) is generic. It does not require much creativity to apply the practice to other sectors. The business case and approval process in the NHS is upheld by HM Treasury, the NAO and other external scrutiny bodies as a model of best practice. Much can be learnt from it.

Purpose of FBC

Approval must be sought for the FBC before the scheme proceeds to financial close and contract award. The current delegated limits for approval are shown in Table 6.1. If a scheme is judged to be novel or contentious, approval may be required from HM Treasury regardless of its capital value.

Table 6.1: Approval thresholds

Total capital cost	Approving authority
Greater than £0.25m for NHS trusts with turnover under £30m	OBC and FBC to Regional Office
Greater than £0.6m for NHS trusts with turnover between £30m and £80m	OBC and FBC to Regional Office
Greater than £1m	OBC and FBC to Regional Office for approval. FBC to NHSE Headquarters for sampling (if selected, approval is required from NHSE)
Greater than £4m	OBC and FBC to Regional Office for approval. FBC to NHSE Headquarters for sampling (if selected, approval is required from NHSE and HM Treasury)
Greater than £10m	FBC requires approval from NHSE and HM Treasury
Greater than £50m	FBC requires approval from NHSE, HM Treasury and Ministers from both departments
NHS IM&T projects	
Less than £20m whole-life costs	OBC and FBC requires approval from Regional Office and NHSE Headquarters
Greater than £20m whole-life costs	FBC requires approval from NHSE and HM Treasury

The purpose of the FBC is to summarise the deal which the procuring entity has negotiated and to demonstrate it satisfies the approving bodies' various requirements. It follows that the FBC should not be submitted until all key, price-sensitive, commercial clauses have been negotiated and agreed. Financiers should have commenced their due diligence work before the FBC has been submitted, and should be content with the main elements of the deal. Financial close should be capable of being reached within three months of approval being granted to the FBC. All the key stakeholders must be satisfied with the quality of services which will be provided under the scheme. As a minimum,

1:200 designs must be completed. Financiers will generally expect to see more detailed design, usually 1:50 before they commit themselves to the project. The interest rate assumption underlying the bidder's price should be stated as well as the period for which the price remains valid before it is reassessed. It is prudent to include an interest rate buffer, say 0.5% above the relevant interest rate, in the tariff on which commissioner support is based to allow for possible movements in the tariff in the period leading to financial close.

All the key commercial issues should be agreed before submission of the FBC. These include *force majeure*, termination (for default by the procuring entity and project company), compensation events, relief events, delay events, change of law, step-in rights of funders, market testing, payment mechanism, indexation and options at the end of the contract.

Approval criteria

The FBC must demonstrate that:

1 The investment is set within a clear, strategic context designed to meet the health service needs of the catchment population and deliver the NHS's objectives as outlined in the local HImP, *The New NHS: modern, dependable* and other strategy documents.
2 The objectives for the project are clearly specified and appropriate options are considered for meeting the investment need (including 'do nothing' and 'do minimum' options).
3 Account has been taken of all relevant costs, benefits and risks, and these have been properly assessed and the preferred option demonstrates best value for money (bearing in mind the three value-for-money tests discussed in Chapter 5).
4 A full assessment of the risks surrounding the investment is undertaken, together with suitable sensitivity analysis on key assumptions, and consideration given to how best the risks may be managed.
5 The investment is affordable and is unequivocally supported by commissioners and/or other relevant stakeholders.
6 There is a clear understanding of the procurement process (including the requirements for full compliance with PFI, relevant legislations and securing the best value-for-money outcome).
7 The contract for the services will be developed in full compliance

with the Department's standard form of contract or any variations agreed with the approval body.

8   There is a clear plan for benefits realisation, including a commitment to assign responsibilities for realising benefits to an individual with sufficient authority and resources to deliver the expected benefits.

9   The investment will be managed in a structured manner (PRINCE being the Department's preferred methodology).

10   There is unequivocal commitment from the chief executive, board chairman and other relevant senior managers, and clear understanding of their continuing roles in the procurement, implementation and benefits realisation process.

11   There is a commitment to post-project evaluation and suitable arrangements are developed to disseminate the results to the authority approving the business case.

12   The investment is clearly presented and is internally consistent.

In addition to these generic criteria, there are a number of specific criteria which are applicable to IM&T investments:

13   Security and confidentiality issues are addressed in accordance with the Bellingham and Caldicott principles.

14   There is sufficient and adequately skilled IM&T resource to manage successfully the specification, procurement and implementation of the services.

15   There is a resourced and structured training programme.

Note, these approval criteria are consistent with the criteria adopted by the NAO in their value-for-money studies. For example, in their review of the first four privately funded DBFO roads (*see* NAO 1998), the issues addressed in their report included:

*   the way the department conducted the negotiations leading up to the award of the contract and whether the approach could be expected to produce best value for money
*   the way risks are identified, allocated, assessed, priced and managed
*   the assessment of value for money and the extent to which the economic appraisal conforms to the technical conventions outlined in HM Treasury's 'Green Book'
*   the management and post-implementation review arrangements for the project. Will services be delivered as required by the contract, and at what cost to the public purse?

Structure of FBC

Although there is no set format for the FBC, it is important for the case to address all the issues which have a direct bearing on the various approval criteria. To facilitate speedy assessment, it is also important for the case to be presented clearly and logically. The arguments, analyses, assumptions and figures should also be internally consistent.

A suggested model is to present the case in five discrete, but complementary, sections along with an executive summary:

1 the strategic case
2 the economic case
3 the financial case
4 the commercial case
5 the project management case.

Note, each of these components can be mapped directly on to the approval criteria outlined above. For example, criteria (2), (3), (4) and (6) are likely to be violated if the economic case has not been soundly developed.

The executive summary summarises the key features of the scheme and deal. This could include:

• the background and objectives of the scheme
• a brief description of the preferred option and its costs
• the results of the procurement process and composition of the consortium
• the results of the economic and financial appraisals
• milestones and timetable to contract award and delivery of services.

Strategic case

The strategic case makes the case for change and outlines the planning context within which the scheme will be developed. For schemes in the health sector this should make explicit reference to the relevant HImP, Ministerial policy imperatives for the NHS and other national, regional and local priorities. It should be developed in conformity with the guidance in phase one of the *Capital Investment Manual* (NHSE 1999).

Issues to address include:

- description of the trust
- trust's business objectives
- background to the scheme
- the case for change
- service models considered
- impact of the scheme on the local health economy
- catchment population
- review of current activity and performance
- forecast of demand for services
- conclusion.

Economic case

The economic case aims to identify the preferred option. This should be based on the results of a rigorous economic appraisal and quantified risk analysis. All key assumptions should be tested in appropriate sensitivity analyses. The preferred option should satisfy all three value-for-money tests discussed in Chapter 5 if 'best' value for money is to be obtained. In some departments, where the use of PSCs is the exception rather than the norm, there is a willingness to accept 'good' value for money, i.e. best PFI option rather than 'best' value for money, i.e. most cost-effective solution, even if this results in funding the project with exchequer capital.

Issues to present in this part of the FBC include:

- summary of the results of the work carried out at the OBC stage
- review of the OBC option appraisal and confirmation that the preferred option identified at OBC stage remains valid
- description of the public sector comparator and confirmation it provides an appropriate comparison for gauging value for money relative to the best PFI option
- brief summary of the PFI procurement process from OJEC to selection of preferred partner
- description of the PFI solution
- build-up of costs of the PFI solution including details of indexation mechanism, proposed funding, extent to which this is agreed with funders, lending terms, financing model and key assumptions (inflation, interest rate, margins, hedging policy, taxation, length of contract, term of debt, unitary payment, cover ratios, etc.)

- methodology and assumptions adopted for economic appraisal and risk analysis
- results of economic appraisal (risk-adjusted NPCs under pessimistic, most likely and optimistic scenarios and sensitivity analyses)
- results of the risk negotiations in the form of a risk allocation matrix
- choice of preferred option and economic rationale for it.

Financial case

This aims to demonstrate the affordability of the preferred value-for-money option. It should assess the revenue impact of both the PSC and PFI option on the procuring entity's income and expenditure account, balance sheet and cashflow position. The financial case should also be unequivocally supported by the main commissioners of the procuring entity's services or those who hold the budget for the services in question.
   It should address:

- assumptions and methodology for the affordability analysis
- description of all sources of income to the procuring entity
- description of the cost of providing services – including the scheme
- details of savings generated from the scheme (e.g. efficiency savings and savings from reduced overheads)
- net affordability impact of the scheme
- VAT treatment of the scheme
- treatment of land and buildings
- results of sensitivity tests on all key assumptions
- accounting treatment of scheme (underpinned by appropriate opinion letters).

Commercial case

This summarises the proposed contract structure and aims to demonstrate that it complies with the official policy and principles outlined in the Department's and Treasury Task Force's standard contract terms. The main provisions of the contract should be described, together with an outline of what has been agreed and what terms remain outstanding.
   It should include:

- confirmation that the standard form of contract is being used
- description of the contractual framework of the proposed scheme, including any variations to standard contract
- description of the provisions of the various agreements (including payment mechanism, indexation, market testing and benchmarking, risk transfer, change of law, delay events, relief events, *force majeure* events, compensation events, consequences and remedies for these various events, termination and step-in rights of funders and procuring entity, length of agreement, break options, options at the end of each break point and expiry of contract – including costs involved, corrupt gifts, employment and TUPE provision, treatment of surplus land, etc.)
- description and diagrammatic representation of the legal relationships between the various parties to the deal
- completed contract matrix to demonstrate compliance with the approving body's/Treasury Task Force's preferred position on the various clauses
- details of how risks transferred to the private sector are embodied in particular contract clauses with direct linkage to the risk allocation matrix.

Project management case

This section of the case is designed to address the critical success factors for the scheme and to demonstrate that robust mechanisms have been put in place to realise the expected benefits.

It should set out details on:

- the overall project management and control arrangements for managing the contract throughout the construction and operation phases of the scheme
- roles and responsibilities of the key members or individual teams (including those drawn from the procuring organisation and the consortium)
- diagrammatic representation of the proposed management structure (from board level down to user working groups)
- the benefit realisation plan (including description of benefits, baseline, targets, measurement indicators, actions and responsibilities for realisation, realisation date, review date, etc.)
- risk management strategy for all risks retained by the public sector during the various stages of the project (*see* Chapter 4)

- details of how the risk management plan will be resourced and implemented
- human resource, communication and change management plan (particularly important in schemes which involve significant changes to the numbers and mix of staff employed). The plan should demonstrate that the service providers will comply with all existing public sector personnel policies and procedures. Any new policies should be no less favourable to the transferred employees
- monitoring and post-project evaluation plan (roles and responsibilities for evaluation, timing, resourcing, issues to be addressed, reporting arrangements and submission date, proposed use and dissemination of findings, etc.)
- resource implications for project management, monitoring and evaluation.

Other issues

The business case should also address any other issues which are considered to be relevant to the scheme and the approval decision, and which do not fit logically in the structure outlined in this chapter. This typically includes:

- timetable to financial close and delivery of services
- information technology and how this will be taken forward if it is not already a component of the scheme. The justification for the proposed procurement route should be provided in the case. If IM&T is included in the scheme, a separate business case is not required provided the IM&T component falls within the procuring entity's delegated limits. If IM&T will be procured separately, a separate business case should be developed. This should comply fully with HSG(95)48 or its replacement. The business case for the main project should also assess the affordability implications of the IM&T subproject to demonstrate that the scheme as a whole is viable
- equipment strategy and how this will be provided. Like IM&T, this may be included or separated from the main project. In both cases, however, the proposed approach should have a clear economic and affordability rationale, and should be explicitly addressed in the business case. The case should explain how any equipment which will be provided outside of the scheme will be funded. It should demonstrate full compliance with appendix 5 of *The Equipping of*

Construction Schemes (see Capital Investment Manual 1994 book-let on The Management of Construction Schemes).

Contract award

Before awarding the contract, it is good practice to update the value-for-money and affordability analyses. The longer the period which elapses between FBC approval and financial close, the more important this requirement becomes.

The usual areas of interest include possible changes in the scope of the project, the quantity and quality of services, risk allocation, any other price-sensitive aspects of the deal and any factor which could affect the accounting treatment for the scheme. Once the relevant analyses have been updated, the results should be shared with the body which approved the FBC. This could be done in the form of an addendum.

Conclusion

This chapter concludes with tips on the preparation and presentation of the FBC:

- involve advisers early in the process, including those with responsibility for approval
- make sure the case includes a clear executive summary
- make sure the case complies with all relevant departmental guidelines and publications
- avoid premature submission of the case
- obtain written and unequivocal support to underpin the various parts of the case (including support from board members, host commissioners, professional opinion from auditors, estates personnel, etc.)
- make sure the value-for-money and risk analyses are updated before awarding the contract. The approving body for the FBC should be notified of any change before the award is made
- make sure the case is presented clearly
- figures and assumptions cited throughout the case should be internally consistent
- all assumptions underlying the various analyses (particularly eco-

nomic appraisal, risk and affordability) should be evidence-based and tested via appropriate sensitivity analyses
- avoid double counting and appraisal optimism
- spurious public sector comparators and risk analyses will be rejected
- the non-financial aspects of the case (e.g. post-project evaluation) are just as important as the financial issues (economic appraisal and affordability analysis)
- ensure the case is submitted to the relevant officials and in the right quantity to avoid unnecessary delay in the approval process
- provide a contact point to deal with queries on the case
- ensure all necessary letters of support and documentation are appended (e.g. OJEC notice, purchaser support letters)
- ensure the case is signed off internally by Board members or the relevant decision makers before it is submitted for approval
- before signing the case off, ensure the various approval criteria outlined in this chapter have been fully satisfied
- ensure project management and control arrangements (including risk management, benefit realisation, contract management and post-implementation review) are properly addressed and resourced.

CHAPTER SEVEN

Case study 1: PFI procurement of a new district general hospital

The new £77m hospital with 579 in-patient beds, currently under construction in Halifax, is the fifth major new hospital to be procured under the PFI. Written largely by Hadyn Cook, Chief Executive of Calderdale Healthcare NHS Trust, this chapter provides a case study of how the scheme was planned and the process leading to commercial and financial close. Emphasis is placed on generic lessons to guide future procurements.

Brief description of the Trust

West Yorkshire is comprised of a number of mill towns, each in separate valleys, with strong distinctive histories. Leeds is the tertiary centre, accessed via the M62 motorway. The local health authority is Calderdale and Kirklees HA, based in Huddersfield, serving a population of around 600 000, spread between Dewsbury, Huddersfield and Halifax as the major population centres.

Calderdale Healthcare NHS Trust provides acute and community services to the population of the Calder Valley. The population of 200 000 is spread between Halifax town, the Upper Valley, including Hebden Bridge, and the Lower Valley, which includes Brighouse. The Trust has a current annual income of over £80m and a stable financial record.

The Trust has responsibility for three hospitals, with the General Hospital and the Royal Infirmaries in Halifax each being around 100 years old. The third hospital is a 1970s 'low rise' flat-roofed building, serving longer stay patients, and based in Northowram, which is four miles from Halifax. The General Hospital provides medical services and the Infirmary the surgical services.

This configuration, coupled with the poor quality of the capital stock, makes it difficult for the Trust to be fully responsive to patients' needs and to achieve the level of clinical effectiveness and service quality it has the potential to attain. The general consensus was that without a new hospital, Calderdale would end up without district general hospital facilities and be reduced to community hospital status. There was a strong local fear that this would result in Huddersfield becoming the main hospital for the local population.

Planning the procurement

The procurement approach adopted by the Trust was broadly consistent with the model outlined in Chapter 3. For the most part, the approach worked well: the Trust successfully passed each approval stage – both government approvals and private sector 'due diligence' activities.

However, the initial emphasis on just specifying 'outcomes' evolved into a joint recognition that firm design detail was needed for the various approvals. Initially, it was thought a specification should be prepared independent of financial constraints, and the advice was that shortlisting should be done regardless of the cost of bids. This was something that was side-stepped.

The specification was reviewed, based on the 'best guess' of likely tender figures, and made sure that the Trust only went out to tender for something it could broadly afford. The Trust subsequently made 'affordability' a shortlisting criterion to ensure it selected a consortium that had a good value-for-money scheme which was also affordable.

The specification

Considerable thought and effort went into the production of the OBS and the underlying service model. At a practical level it was necessary to get it right. The Trust recognised that with PFI it would be 'locked into' a contract for 30 years.

The Trust commissioned York University to help undertake the analytical work to scope the OBS and determine the size of the facility.

This took into account demographic factors, medical advances, patients' expectations, current performance on bed management and a host of other determinants of healthcare provision. The Trust tried to avoid aiming for 'upper decile' performance, although a later squeeze on beds pushed it in that direction.

Conscious that requirements will change over time, flexibility was also a key component to the scheme, and a formal change/variation mechanism was built into the contract to achieve change at reasonable cost. The health authority then used independent advisers to verify and challenge the original results from the modelling work. Later, the consortium's bankers, as part of their 'due diligence' work, ran a similar check.

The modelling was mainly based on projections over time. It also considered 'peaks and troughs' by analysing current day-by-day occupancy by specialty. It included graphs of trends by specialty that will need to be achieved to deliver the planned bed numbers. This work also helped to specify the necessary number of theatres, day beds and out-patient consulting rooms.

Much of the rest of the specification was based on traditional NHS norms. The proposals that were received proved to be broadly in line with these, but with reduced areas in some departments. Various pieces of work were later done to prove these proposals, such as ward 'mock-ups' to check their viability.

Project approach and PFI process

As part of the process of producing the OBC, the Trust undertook an assessment to determine whether the project was suitable to be delivered by the private sector. The conclusion was favourable and the OJEC was placed on 22 June 1995 (*see* Box 7.1). A Project Board was formed by the Trust (*see* Box 7.2) using PRINCE methodology. This included medical consultants, general practitioners, the Vice-Chairman, Chief Executive, Director of Finance, a number of other executive and non-executive directors, and the Director of Planning of Calderdale and Kirklees Health Authority.

It was recognised from the outset that substantial management time would be required. The volume of paperwork subsequently produced attests to this. A new Chief Executive was appointed in February 1996; by the autumn it was evident that the project needed total commitment from the whole top management team if it was to succeed.

Box 7.1: OJEC advertisement

UK-Halifax: hospital buildings
(95/S 124-64128/EN)

1 **Awarding authority**: Calderdale Healthcare NHS Trust, Royal Halifax Infirmary, Free School Lane, UK-Halifax HX1 2YP
(Tel: 01422 357222, Fax: 01422 342581)
Mr Doug Farrow, Acting Chief Executive

2(a) **Site**: Halifax General Hospital, Salterhebble, UK-Halifax HX3 0PW
 (b) **Subject of concession**: CPV 45211541

The award authority currently provides a full range of hospital and community services and now wishes to consolidate all hospital services on to the Halifax General Hospital site with a development of a new facility to serve the population of UK-Calderdale (circa 200 000), and intends to test the viability of a private sector option in line with the Government's Private Finance Initiative. This will include substantial new build and probably an element of refurbishment. The proposal has received Outline Business Case approval.

The work comprises the redevelopment of UK-Calderdale's hospital facilities and it is not expected that the tender will be divided into lots, although in the absence of comprehensive bids from suitable parties or consortia, division into lots may be considered.

Expressions of interest are invited for the design, construction, financing and, where appropriate, equipping of the development, on land provided by the Trust, in return for a concession, whose terms will include the opportunity to provide the Trust with facilities management of the development, including the provision of a range of non-core services.

3(a) **Deadline for receipt of applications**: 8.9.1995
 (b) **Address**: As in 1.
  Following the above date, a number of parties or consortia will be shortlisted to negotiate.
 (c) **Language(s)**: English

4 **Qualifications**: To be fulfilled by the candidates, each applicant and, in the case of the consortia, each member must provide:
• banker's reference

- balance sheet, together with any statement of accounts for the last three financial years
- statement of overall turnover and turnover on construction works and services relevant to the nature of the contract for the previous three years
- details of education and professional qualifications of managerial staff and of those who will have specific responsibility for the matters covered by the proposed concession contract in previous three years, accompanied by certificates of satisfactory execution
- an indication of the technicians or technical bodies who can be called upon.

Parties and consortia are further required to demonstrate their financial and technical suitability for the award of the concession, but addressing additional matters as set out in the pre-qualification document (see 7).

5 **Award criteria (other than price)**: The intention is to award the concession contract through a competitive negotiated procedure. The criteria for the award will be based on what is economically most advantageous to the Trust, having regard to factors likely to include price, quality and appropriateness of the development and of service provision, flexibility, period for completion and the conformity of contractors' proposals to the requirements of the UK Government's Private Finance Initiative.

6 **Subcontract**: Candidates should indicate what proportion of the value of the works they are likely to award to third parties. They should also indicate which service elements of the contract they propose to subcontract.

7 **Other information**: A pre-qualification document giving further information as to the appointment process and outlining the scope of the works and potential contracts is available from Mrs Sue Ellis, address as in 1, who should also be contacted by anyone wishing to visit the briefing room which has been set up at the Royal Halifax Infirmary.

8 **Notice postmarked**: 22.6.1995

9 **Notice received on**: 22.6.1995

Box 7.2: The Project Board

The Trust chose to involve the whole executive team as the project team.

Person	Role
Project Director	Project management
Chief Executive	Negotiations
Finance Director	Finance, IT
Director of Operations	Design and construction
Chief Nurse	Equipment
Director of HR	Support services
Board Secretary	Legal issues

One of the early tasks of the Project Board was to appoint external advisers. This was done by competitive tendering and resulted in the appointment of Price Waterhouse as financial advisers, Llewelyn-Davies as healthcare planning/technical design advisers, Yorkshire Food Services as support for development of service specifications and Nabarro Nathanson as legal advisers. Expenditure on advisers was tightly controlled. In-house legal expertise was utilised as far as possible.

A briefing room was set up at the Royal Halifax Infirmary to house information about the project, and which was made available to all potential bidders. Following the OJEC advertisement, those expressing an interest in the project were sent a document entitled 'Information for Candidates Applying to Pre-qualify'. In the pre-qualification documentation, it was made clear that shortlisting would be restricted to those able to offer a DBFO solution. There were 13 general expressions of interest and five submissions for pre-qualification. The ITN was issued to four consortia. The deadline for the return of bids was 4 March 1996.

The information provided to the consortia built on what was previously included in the pre-qualification material. It made clear that their solutions should accommodate the following:

- a continuing increase in acute admissions
- a reduction in length of stay
- a transfer of some services to community settings and primary care
- an increase in the provision of higher technologically based care with a transfer of some services from tertiary centres to locally provided care in the new development.

With regard to the design and construction requirements, they were encouraged to propose innovative solutions rather than merely adopting the Trust's design ideas. This was informed by a series of operational policies which had been worked on by teams internally and a description of the overall functional content required.

The output specification for each of the support services was provided to each consortium. Care was taken not to impose unnecessary constraints on bidders. This was partly achieved by providing a general description of the outputs required, service-specific definition and the desired standards.

Following intensive discussions with the four consortia and a formal evaluation, only two of the four consortia were shortlisted to proceed to the Invitation to Tender stage (ITT). At this stage, the Trust was able to engage in more detailed discussions around its requirements. This was reflected in the ITT documentation which was issued on 25 May 1996. Standard bids were sought from both consortia based on a requirement of 612 in-patient beds. The number of theatres required was not specified. The shortlisted parties were also given the opportunity to submit variant bids. A submission date of 7 August 1996 allowed for the consortia to visit the Trust and allowed for a period of clarification, evaluation and negotiation. Following evaluation of the bids and interviews, a preferred bidder was announced on 6 September 1996.

Evaluation model and selection of preferred bidder

The Trust carried out a formal evaluation of bids at each stage, not only to ensure that it identified the best bid(s), but also to ensure the process was defensible if challenged. The Trust also offered debriefs at each stage for unsuccessful bidders.

Supported by our advisers, an evaluation model was developed to be used at each stage in the procurement process. The evaluation criteria at pre-qualification included: contract framework and risk (weighted 18), capability – building and design (weighted 18), capability – service providers (weighted 28), continuing consortium arrangements (weighted 18) and financial proposals (weighted 18). At each stage bids were scored against each criterion. The weight applied to each criterion was based on the project team's assessment of their relative importance. A total weighted score was then calculated for each bid.

The highest bidders at each stage went through to the next round. A member of the project team led on each issue, with technical support provided by the external advisers.

At ITN, the Trust added criteria about equipment, supplies and IT (low weighting) and affordability (high weighting). In effect, the latter was intended to ensure that the Trust was only finally shortlisting proposals that it could afford. At ITT, the Trust carried out a separate evaluation of the non-financial aspects of the bids based on: contract terms, design/facilities and support services.

Catalyst (the Bovis consortium) submitted a 'variant bid', which retained more existing estate. This scored higher than the competitor, and was also cheaper on the financial evaluation.

A formal value-for-money and affordability analysis was undertaken. The latter took into account the capital charge and the proposed service costs, discounted back to net present cost over the full-term period. Detailed sensitivity analysis was also undertaken, including testing weights and scores.

Overall the Catalyst consortium offered the better tender and was appointed as the preferred bidder. However, further work had to be done to make the bid affordable. Some of this was done by reducing soft facilities management costs, devising an innovative way of funding the scheme which reduced the annual payments and finding more money to fund the scheme. Equally the Trust deliberately left a gap until financial close, knowing that if it found more money and put it on the table, there was a danger that another 'gap' could appear.

Once selected as preferred partner, Catalyst formalised their consortium. The special purpose non-recourse company included Bovis, RCO and British Linen Bank. They provided evidence of banking and equity support. A banking consortium of several banks progressed the scheme, but eventually this narrowed down to the Halifax Bank and the Bank of Scotland actually funding the scheme. Hambro's (now Société Generale) joined later as the equity provider.

At the request of Catalyst, the Trust made a presentation to prospective financiers about the prospects of the scheme. This occurred at the ITN stage. It was felt this engagement with the banks should begin early.

Content of scheme

Originally the guidance was that the Trust should just specify outputs (Finished Consultant Episodes, etc.) and the private sector would use its ingenuity to deliver a cost-effective solution. In reality the Trust had to specify more clearly (e.g. bed numbers), and the banks would only loan money against a clearly designed and costed scheme which had the Trust's 'sign off'.

Bovis Facilities Management have a 30-year contract for building and engineering maintenance, along with life-cycle replacements (i.e. hard facilities management services). RCO have a 30-year contract for support services, including catering, portering, domestics, laundry, security, car parking and stores delivery (i.e. soft facilities management services).

The Trust chose not to include much by way of equipment in the deal to ensure affordability. The Trust is therefore mainly transferring equipment from existing hospitals into the new hospital. Existing IM&T likewise is being transferred into the new hospital on grounds of affordability. A decision to adopt digital technology (rather than build the wet film processing facilities into the new X-ray department), means that the Trust is pursuing a parallel business case for a patient administration system. The information services business case will comply fully with the strategic requirements of the new information strategy *Information for Health* published by the DoH in 1998.

Business cases

'Approval in principle' for a major development was granted by the Department of Health in 1986, but capital funding was not available at that time. In 1993 work was done on a revised 'approval in principle', and further to this an OBC was submitted to the Regional Office by the newly established Calderdale Healthcare NHS Trust. This received Regional approval in December 1994.

The OBC considered a 'longlist' of ten options, including 'do nothing', refurbishment and the greenfield site option.

Non-financial criteria were applied, which included:

- accessibility
- quality of clinical care

- acceptability to staff
- quality of estate.

Financial criteria were also used, which included:

- affordability
- net present cost and annual equivalent cost
- ability to finance the scheme
- generation of funds for reinvestment.

These were shortlisted as follows: do nothing, do minimum, a single-site option and a two-site option. The do minimum option entailed:

- hospital services on two sites
- closure and disposal of the surplus site
- elderly and mental health wards moved from Northowram hospital (the surplus site)
- improved premises with maintenance standards to Estate code category B
- minor capital expenditure
- reduction in beds to accommodate all activity on two sites
- investment in community services to accommodate the transfer of activity from the acute settings.

The economic appraisal demonstrated that only the 'single-site' option gave significant savings. In addition, the results demonstrated that failure to concentrate on a single site would leave the Trust with the additional costs and inefficiencies associated with running hospitals at several sites, inflexibility around the use of beds, antiquated clinical care and the necessity of spending capital monies on backlog maintenance to the tune of £52.1m (1996 prices) to achieve statutory standards – particularly essential safety works.

The single-site option was, therefore, accepted as the preferred option. At this stage, it was viewed as a 'public sector comparator'. Before testing for PFI, the Trust and health authority led a consultation exercise to gauge the acceptability of a single-site solution to the catchment population and other stakeholders. The main concern expressed was about the adequacy of bed numbers in the proposal.

Once the preferred partner was selected and all price-sensitive aspects of the contract were negotiated, a FBC was prepared to determine the best method of funding for the project. Although not a viable option, the do minimum option was retained to serve as a further benchmark for gauging value for money. However, the main value-for-money comparison was between Catalyst's PFI bid and the updated public sector comparator. The PSC was updated to reflect changes in services, bed numbers, functional content, building cost inflation and regulations, and the value of risk retained by the public sector under this option. VAT and capital charges were excluded. Equipment and IS/IT were also excluded to ensure a fair comparison with the PFI option.

The economic and financial appraisal conclusively demonstrated the superiority of the PFI option on value for money and affordability grounds. It involved:

- single-site development incorporating all hospital services
- disposal of the two surplus sites
- all building stock upgraded to at least Estmancode category B
- concept space planning producing operational efficiency gains
- effective vertical circulation producing a 'tight' building layout with minimised horizontal circulation
- the majority of clinical services provided from new building stock
- site configuration designed to ensure that the existing hospital buildings are effectively integrated into the development thereby facilitating efficient operational policies
- comprehensive site roadway layouts incorporating dedicated entrances for emergency and goods vehicles
- nursing unit concepts (informed by discussion with local care groups)
- a secure and 'patient friendly' environment
- a reduced building programme (thereby reducing overall capital required and producing revenue savings earlier)
- integration of clinical specialties to reduce clinical support service costs
- substantial flexibility in the future use of the building (to contract or to expand as required).

The Full Business Case document

The FBC document kept returning to haunt us. The Trust had a first go at it prior to the general election, got approval after the election and then final approval just before contract close.

It is a major document, in the public domain, outlining the history of the scheme, the process and the recommendations. It includes chapters on the estate, the finances, legal matters and so on.

The Trust knew that good presentation would be helpful. The main document was a thick, A4 lever arch file full of papers, along with sets of drawings, the draft contract and financial appendices. The Trust chose to have some covers printed – in a different colour for each edition – and had a box made to contain complete sets. The Trust usually produced around 30 copies – and invariably, so it seemed, by means of the executive team working into the night to do the photo-copying, hole punching and collating.

The Trust was aware that the main document would be a public one, but would need a confidential annex to present the confidential information, mainly relating to the 'commercial in confidence' tender price and breakdown. The Trust has since made copies publicly available; apart from some academic interest, the main reader, as far as the Trust is aware, has been the Unison local full-time official, who was naturally concerned about issues relating to employment and support services.

Benefits realisation is an area of the submission where the Trust particularly struggled. The Trust is signed up to the concept of identi-fying benefits and managing their achievement: for example this needs a project plan and baseline data. However, the Trust found it hard to be clear as to what was wanted, and as the 'final part' of the project and FBC it took us some time to deliver this to a satisfactory standard.

Negotiating the contract

The Trust negotiated almost continuously with Catalyst from September 1996 through to July 1998. Some of that time was spent on commercial issues and other non-legal issues, but the Trust got snared into an overwhelming and protracted legal negotiation.

Most meetings seemed to involve lawyers, and the legal contract seemed to be the basic agenda for almost every meeting. Arguably this suited us, as it distracted from the commercial negotiations, but incurred huge legal costs. In retrospect the Trust should have at least tried to debate the issues through to a resolution, and then find appropriate legal words, rather than trying to refine legal wording of clauses, where inevitably the lawyers had to take a lead role. As such the agenda was very much taken out of the Trust's hands.

The legal negotiations went on *ad nauseam*, with about 30 drafts of the contract being produced (the Trust regularly lost track of which revision it was working on). The non-lawyers began to get an under-standing of the legal points and debate, and became very familiar with the editing system that identified changes from previous drafts (i.e. additions, deletions).

Legal points

Much of the legal debate revolved around issues of risk transfer. Catalyst wanted to minimise the risk transfer to them, and the banks and their lawyers were even more averse to accepting almost any risk transfer. Much of this was irrational, in that nobody seemed to want to put a financial or even statistical value on these risks (i.e. how much is it worth, how likely is it to happen). Nobody seemed to want to engage in a debate about saying that the risk could be shifted for an appropriate price.

In practice, the Trust got into frequent stand-offs, where it seemed that the private sector strategy was simply to try to 'water down' the contract and hope that the Trust could be worn down into making concessions to make progress.

In the early days there was little guidance as to what was acceptable: in due course the Centre produced 'tramlines' which provided guidance on key issues. At the same time each deal that closed provided emerging precedents but with the private sector not surprisingly 'cherry picking' and quoting the best parts of every other deal.

At one stage the Trust suggested migrating major parts of the Trust contract to that for another deal if the private sector really wanted the whole, i.e. the good and the bad parts, of the other deal.

Timescale

The time taken to close the scheme was disappointingly long. At times it felt as if the other side was deliberately going for a 'war of attrition' with a view to wearing us down. However, generally they were arguing small points, increasing their own legal costs and delaying the scheme. As such, they were also increasing their general financial exposure over time.

Rationally it did not seem like a considered strategy of theirs, more a lack of project management skills, along with a very cautious approach. Arguably, construction is a risky business, PFI is new and therefore some caution is justifiable.

The banks' involvement added to the time taken. In part, their revisiting of the legal agreement, with their lawyers, added further rounds of negotiation. In parallel, their 'due diligence' requirements to review all aspects of the scheme proved to be a protracted process, particularly when Bovis had to carry out further design work to satisfy their requirements.

The Trust tried various devices to get everybody to move more quickly. It was tempting to issue ultimata, but the Trust would have lost credibility if its bluff had been called (and everybody knew the Trust couldn't go anywhere else). To be fair, the consortium had a more complex job than us, in terms of dealing with subcontractors, banks and various other bodies as well as with us.

Towards financial close the PFU made available some 'tramline guidelines' which outlined the Department's preferred position on a number of the key contractual clauses. This proved very useful to the Trust: it reduced the amount of time and costs which would otherwise be expended on negotiating the various clauses of the contract.

The tramlines included: definition of *force majeure*, change in law (including legislative changes which have a revenue and capital cost impact), delay and compensation events, relief events, compensation in the event of *force majeure* termination, compensation in the event of NHS trust default, how to deal with project company default, provision of the payment mechanism, indexation, benchmarking and market testing, transfer of third party equity and the policy on TUPE matters.

Once the Department's position was specified, it was then a matter for final negotiation to try to get the private sector's (especially banks) agreement to these points, and then reach a final compromise on a final few points. At this stage the PFU gave the Trust close support, including attending meetings to help finalise these matters.

Interestingly the PFU staff included a range of secondees from the private sector – particularly lawyers and accountants – with quite a high turnover, but a real willingness to help make things happen. However, PFI in healthcare is quite a small world, and occasionally positions were taken by individuals, on all sides, which were known to be at variance with positions on recent deals in which they had been involved. Similarly, some consultants were currently working for both the NHS and the private sector on different schemes but representing opposite sides. This needs to be managed carefully. It can easily lead to conflicts of interest.

Key elements of the contract

The legal contract is a means of reflecting the commercial understanding – or so it was thought! There were times when it felt like it was an end in itself – no matter if the hospital did not work, as long as the legal words were sound. The inclination, each time the Trust had a legal debate, was to try to put a commercial value on the issue (what's the cost, how likely is it to happen) and also put a cost on the legal time spent resolving the issue (is it worth spending several thousand pounds an hour resolving trivia).

All the Trust's lawyers tended to shroud wave and it is hard to go against legal advice. The major meetings had both the Trust's and Catalyst's lawyers present. Often the banks' lawyers would be involved. This sometimes included a general lawyer and a specialist lawyer (construction, employment, pensions, leases, etc.). For some of the time, in-house or retained lawyers for Bovis and RCO were also involved.

One meeting at Clifford Chance, close to financial close, had around 20 people present. The lawyers were typically getting £300 an hour. The total cost of the time involved must have been in the order of £3600 an hour, or £1 per second. Given that the Trust was paying all of this (through reimbursing their start-up costs if it proceeded to contract close) this concentrated the mind. To be told that costs had increased, due to delays that the Trust felt were due to the other side, and that the Trust had to meet them, was a cause of considerable aggravation.

Legal

The Trust's lawyers drafted a complex contract, reflecting the nature of the deal, and achieved the necessary performance requirements and risk transfer. The eternal negotiations changed some elements, either substantially or trivially, but which generated much work in flowing these through to the other relevant clauses.

Special purpose vehicle

A basic principle was that the private sector group would establish a shell company to run the scheme. This took the scheme 'off balance sheet' for them, minimising the impact on their balance sheets. Later, however, they had to give substantial covenants to the banks (i.e. offering guarantees about aspects of the SPV's business) which must have diluted this benefit.

The SPV incorporated equity (10% initially, but this was diluted by cheaper mezzanine debt) so that it had investment at risk, receiving high rates of return, but in principle enabling it to accept risks.

The Trust could only justify the higher cost of private sector borrowing if it could demonstrate that risk transfer and other efficiencies from their solution made the scheme worthwhile. Risk transfer was, therefore, crucial. Ironically it then turned out that the banks were not only risk averse, but did not want the SPV to overexpose itself to risk even if the risks were controllable. Nobody wanted to take the risk that there might be 'consecrated land' and human remains found during construction. To be fair, more risk absorption might have been possible, but at a greater cost, and part of the Trust's burden was to keep the scheme comparable to a 'public sector option' which was relatively low cost.

Payment mechanism

PFI only gets schemes 'off balance sheet' for the Trust if a 'serviced building' is provided and a variable payment stream is paid for that facility. Ideally this should be a 'unitary payment stream' which reduces to 'zero for zero availability'. In practice, the banks wanted to be able to see the element of payment that covered their lending and to ensure it was relatively secure.

The payment mechanism therefore consisted of three elements, with part linked to assessed quality and volume. These were called the availability-, performance- and volume-related elements. Availability amounts to roughly 55% of the total and performance accounted for 40%. This effectively shifts the service quality risk to the private sector.

Officially the Trust was not interested in the build cost (the Trust 'just specifies outcomes and pays for the serviced building'). However, in order to evaluate and control the total payment cost, it was helpful to monitor the build cost, and in fact most of the Trust's negotiations about costs revolved around the reasonableness of the build cost. This was only possible because the Trust had managed to incorporate an 'open book' clause in the agreement.

The build cost was a constant problem since the Trust could barely afford the cost. Moreover, Bovis were very wary of the 'fixed cost' nature of the contract – as long as the Trust avoids 'client variations' they have to do the job for the fixed price (their contract is actually with Catalyst and funded by the banks). Sometimes it felt as if they were trying to take the profit on variations before they happened, and they seemed to have large risk margins. However, the public sector comparator was based on 25% to 33% costs overruns which had been the public sector tradition (and therefore the previous basis for builders' prices).

Force majeure

The Trust's team became transient experts in what appears to be arcane legal points. The Trust spent hours debating variations on the 'act of God' theme, where costs are incurred but for which neither party is to blame. An example was 'off-site utility failure', where failure of supply could result in non-availability of the building (e.g. through being unheated); in that situation should the Trust still pay the SPV or abate the payment?

Some of these events were currently insurable (e.g. terrorism); the Trust had to debate what to do if they became uninsurable (at reasonable cost). The banks said that 'termination' might be necessary, since they could not lend money against a building that did not have full insurance cover if it was damaged.

Termination

Termination of the agreement, by the fault of either party, is a major issue. An example of an issue is the question of the extent to which their shareholders should be compensated in certain cases for future loss of dividends.

Employment/TUPE

Employment issues, linked to the transfer of support services, deserves a book in its own right. The Trust had to consider the details of the transfer, in the TUPE context, and what should happen about pay increases between now and the transfer of staff.

There were a number of issues about the period from contract close to services commencement when the facilities management staff remain in the Trust's employ. The consortium wanted reassurance that their costs would not increase due to NHS pay rises (they claimed their prices were based on current NHS rates) and that the Trust would not upgrade staff before protected TUPE transfer. They also wanted the Trust to only transfer the staff they required, matching a profile of staff, and to bear the costs of any redundancies and early retirements required to deliver this. Longer term we wanted reassurances about protection for transferred staff, for example in terms of retaining their NHS pensions or something equivalent.

Financial and commercial

The financial issues included the payment mechanism and the financial consequences of termination. It also included income generation issues (how to share the restaurant income/profit), VAT and tax issues.

Inflation

The Trust had to negotiate how to handle indexing (or otherwise) for inflation, in effect over a 30-year agreement. Various indices were selected by interested parties, with Treasury indicating a necessity for a single index and a preference for retail price index (RPI) or the GDP deflator. The Trust debated the possible variation between RPI and the GDP inflator.

The Trust also agreed 'benchmarking' for soft facilities management services at six-yearly intervals, which should provide a correction mechanism if any key variable gets out of step. Build cost inflation was a constant concern, given that construction industry inflation is above RPI and increasing. This meant that over time Bovis was increasing the cost due to increased differentials in inflation allowances. Delays to the scheme in terms of negotiations were in danger of pushing it financially out of reach.

Interest rates

Interest rates were of great concern, given a worry that they would increase with the change in government – and given that what the Trust paid was significantly dependent on what Catalyst had to pay the banks by way of interest.

The Trust considered buying a 'hedge' against interest rate increase. This would have cost almost £1m. The Trust would have liked to have done it, but were told that they should not 'gamble' on interest rates. As it happened, interest rates actually reduced, and played a key part in the final affordability debate.

The Trust also looked at bonds as a possible alternative to bank finance. The Carlisle scheme had used bond finance, and it looked as if it could be quicker and cheaper. However, the Trust established that it had got too far with the banks in its negotiations to make it worthwhile to seriously pursue another source of funding at this late stage. Moreover, the banks were also very flexible and helpful in the closing stages.

Final commercial negotiations

Catalyst had tried to increase the price over time, due to increasing build cost estimates from Bovis. The Trust had kept these negotiations going, without firm conclusions, in order to progress the scheme, and in the belief that any 'final' commercial agreement was worthless until contract close, and would possibly be followed by further cost increases.

Once the Trust got close to contract close it then had some very gritty commercial negotiations. Catalyst were saying they needed around £15.5m a year by way of payment stream, and the Trust said it could afford around £14m. The Trust explained that it had only limited resources and that it could not justify a higher sum in terms of value for money versus the public sector comparator.

The Trust tried to attack its cost make-up, particularly by challenging the detail of the build cost (which determined a large part of the recurrent cost). However, they were resolute in their position, and even 'walk outs' by either side as a negotiating tactic did not bring the sides closer.

The Trust involved the health authority, partly to demonstrate to the consortium that we were speaking with one voice and partly to show the health authority we were trying to keep costs down to an absolute minimum. The health authority managers were quite shocked by the ferocity of some of the negotiations and made aware of the challenge of dealing with 'real money' (money 'leaving the system' as opposed to annual contract negotiations within the NHS where the money is 'recycled' within the system).

By the last two months it should be added that everyone was getting tired – with regular weekend working and long days that often turned into working through the night. Good health and stamina were key elements to keeping the negotiations going. Often points would be conceded in the early hours because everyone had got beyond defending their negotiating positions.

Fortunately the Halifax Bank was very committed to funding the hospital in its home town, and by reviewing its own funding structure was able to offer more helpful terms. Interest rates were also moving in the right direction, which helped to reduce the funding cost, and the Trust and the consortium both managed to make small financial concessions. As such, the Trust was finally able to resolve the financial gap and 'shake hands' on a deal which then held through to the last days of final contract close.

The role of advisers

The advisers played a major role in the procurement process and the closing of the deal. The Trust formally tendered for the appointment of advisers in view of the sums of money involved for fees. In retrospect it would have been better to have regionally based advisers. The distance from Halifax to London was significant in terms of wasted travel time, travel costs, and the sheer wear and tear of travelling along with long working days.

The Trust chose to appoint outside lawyers – a necessary step – but had the good fortune to have an 'in-house' lawyer in the form of a legally qualified Board Secretary. The burden that John Bundock shouldered was immense, but made a real difference to controlling and progressing the scheme.

The Trust also appointed financial advisers. They were used principally to help evaluate bids, produce the economic appraisal, advise on funding options and value for money, and for general commercial and negotiating support. The Trust ended up making major use of a quantity surveyor to try to challenge and control price/cost changes by Bovis. The Trust appointed Llewellyn Davis as architects, who advised mainly on the design process.

The lawyers proved to be the main external cost. We had agreed a discounted hourly rate with them – what they described as 'working at a loss' – and then tried to manage the number of hours worked. In retrospect it might have been worth trying to 'fee cap' the lawyers, but neither side could have accurately anticipated the amount of work or the time taken.

The role of stakeholders

Kirklees and Calderdale Health Authority

The health authority showed support throughout for the scheme, but required the Trust to reduce bed numbers, deliver financial savings, and a shift in expenditure to community services (using the Cash Releasing Efficiency Savings for five years plus £2.5m in savings from the hospital closures). They participated actively in the planning of the scheme throughout the various stages. Their involvement, especially senior managers, was particularly close as the project moved beyond the ITN

stage. This level of support and commitment from the senior management team, including attendance at meetings, strengthened the negotiating position of the Trust with the shortlisted bidders. The few GP
fundholders in Calderdale also provided helpful letters of support.

Consultation with the public

The health authority organised a three-month period of public consultation as part of the OBC process. The closure of Northowram
Hospital was a significant local issue. The project was presented as
the 'redevelopment of services' with community services replacing and
supporting hospital services an integral part of the proposal.

Part of the public consultation was the issue of the reduction in bed
numbers. Everyone had some concern about the tough targets proposed, which have been a requirement for any successful bid. Locally
the issue was complicated by a further wish to examine the possibility
of shifting activity from a hospital to a community setting. As such, 70
beds were held back from the hospital while the health authority
considered whether these could be replaced by community services:
this caused some local concern and provided an opportunity for some
opposition.

Other stakeholders

The local Liberal Party criticised aspects of the scheme both before and
after the general election. The Labour-led local council understood the
need for a new hospital, but with some concerns about PFI as a
principle.

Specific concerns were expressed about the bed reductions and the
commitment to strengthening community services. At one stage it was
feared that a 'judicial review' might be initiated locally. In order to
manage this risk and offer reassurance, a Scrutiny Committee was
established to provide a local forum to discuss the scheme and any local
concerns. This included representatives of the local political parties –
councillors – plus the Trust, health authority and CHC. The CHC was
supportive throughout the project, despite reservations about PFI and
the size of the hospital.

'Campaign against a smaller hospital' ('CASH')

A retired local obstetrician and one-time Liberal councillor formed a small pressure group, consisting mainly of a small group of Liberal colleagues. They were concerned about the bed reductions plus other aspects from time to time. They received a huge amount of coverage locally, mainly because of the 'retired' doctor's credibility.

The Trust chose not to engage in major local debate, fearing that it was difficult to win the argument over public concerns and not wanting to 'raise the temperature'. Specifically, it chose not to engage clinicians to rebut arguments: it did not want them to be caught up in local political debate.

Working with the Regional Office, PFU and HM Treasury

The region worked closely with the PFU to monitor and support the project. The region was unusual in having several schemes in the first wave, and was therefore quite stretched. Part of its role was to check that there was general support for the scheme, particularly by the health authority.

The PFU was very supportive and helpful throughout. Rather than acting as civil servant 'bureaucrats and gatekeepers', it chose to be proactive in its support. It organised occasional formal review meetings, both on the public sector side, and also with the private sector when appropriate. It had a formal role in approving the FBC which it did efficiently, and moved very fast indeed once financial close was imminent.

The NHS Management Executive's approval process included financial reviews of the Trust proposals (shared with region) and economic review. The former involved reviews of affordability, risk transfer and whether the scheme was 'off balance sheet'. The latter included a review of the scheme to compare net present values of the private sector option and the public sector comparator. Again, the relevant officials were effective and supportive throughout.

The Treasury was involved at two levels. The Trust had occasional involvement from the PFI Task Force, and others, which was intended to promote and encourage the PFI approach. These tended to be broad-based reviews which concentrated on issues such as the proposed financing structure and whether it was designed to achieve sufficient risk transfer. Treasury also had a formal role in approving the scheme which it did with characteristic efficiency.

Lessons learned

Importance of good project management

The project management approach is absolutely critical to a successful outcome. The time and effort required to achieve the various milestones should not be underestimated. PFI is a very complex process and needs a focused approach based on the project approach. Some project management training plus one or two people who 'think that way' are important.

The Trust fully involved the executive team rather than having a separate 'project' team. This gave people double workloads (project plus 'day jobs') but meant that the most senior people were driving the project. The Trust had good support from the Trust Chair and the Board. They must be properly informed so that they can make the right input when it is required.

The Trust reviewed its negotiating strategy and constantly reflected on ways and means of expediting progress. The Trust consciously deployed the Trust team to try and establish rapport with the other side, and played to team and individual strengths. Ultimately the Trust simply managed to keep going, which may not be in the PRINCE textbooks, but which made the difference in getting to the finishing line.

The Trust involved its Human Resources Director who had industrial relations negotiating expertise, which was the closest it came to 'commercial' negotiating expertise. The Trust changed tactics from time to time. For example, the Trust found that 'squawkbox' telephone conference calls for a while seemed to achieve more undivided attention and progress than face-to-face meetings in London.

Effective communication

The Trust needs to identify and keep stakeholders and key supporters on board. The Trust tried hard to ensure that the CHC and the local authority felt involved. The Trust chose to work closely with local MPs, who were tremendously supportive.

A regular project meeting involved the various stakeholders, and a formal meeting was established with local authority representatives. The MPs were briefed regularly on their 'constituency days'.

Contract close would not have been achieved were it not for the personal intervention and support of the MPs and their assistants. It is easy to forget times when the Trust was ringing literally everyone it knew to try to keep things moving.

The final week is an amazing culmination of a huge amount of work. The signed documents will fill several crates in the lawyers' offices. Ideally you will keep a final reserve of energy and good humour for this critical stage. For example, the banks had two new senior lawyers working on the project for the last few days since colleagues were away. Coping with financiers challenging fundamental aspects of the deal without understanding the background was enough to try the patience of a saint (and the Trust was, by now, a very tired saint!).

The Trust was asked to make a final concession by the consortium's lawyer, and then one by the bank's lawyer, as dawn approached on the final day. The Trust managed to say to each one: 'the Trust will discuss it if it is really the only issue remaining on the table'. Fortunately they kept their word.

Selecting the preferred partner and advisers

Selecting the private sector partner is a major decision. A part of the process should be spent consciously getting to know the key people and the organisations personally, and getting a sense of what they are like, including the values of their organisations. References should also be obtained from organisations to whom they have previously supplied services. By now, it should be possible to get meaningful references from their involvement in previous PFI schemes, even if it is from outside the health sector.

It is easy to say that negotiations should not be adversarial, but rather should be partnership-based. The conflicts of interest make it naive to assume it can all be easy: the Trust had shouting matches at various stages. The deal certainly will not happen satisfactorily without dedication and some energy or passion. Equally, and towards the end, working together is essential. The Trust was lucky that, however fraught the 'official' relationships, several of us could always talk collaboratively, and a number of difficult issues were resolved over some relatively clandestine breakfast meetings.

Managing advisers

When you shortlist professional advisers you are shortlisting both individuals (partners) and the partnership. The latter matters because it gives you the support in depth. It can be embarrassing if the individual assigned to the scheme does not deliver. On more than one occasion the Trust chose to change the preferred lead person to get the service and support it wanted.

Leading the advisers, particularly the lawyers, rather than being led by them, is difficult but necessary. A member of the team needs to have a feel for the legal issues, and then ideally gives good direction as to how these should be handled and how long to take over them. Sensibly this would be a bilateral effort with the private partner: if a 'standard contract' is developed this may fall away as an issue, but only if everyone is determined to stick to the standard contract.

The Trust spent a substantial amount on consultants' fees, partly because it was a trail-blazing scheme. However, ideally the Trust would have spent less and, with the benefit of hindsight, it should have devised arrangements to reduce these costs further.

However, it is very difficult when the Trust's lead lawyer says he thinks a specialist opinion is required, say from a pensions lawyer. Moreover, at one stage the other side 'fee-capped' their lawyers and part of the Trust's negotiating strength at that time was the fact that the Trust's lawyers could put in more time if necessary.

Keeping control of the contract draft is of some value and both sets of lawyers will try to do this. Asking for a copy of the contract on a floppy disk is a sure sign of this! However, it is something of a poisoned chalice: the Trust was asking for quick turnrounds of drafting, which meant the Trust's lawyers were regularly working through the night after days of sitting in on negotiations. While well paid, there is no denying that their stamina, plus their 'back office' support, is very impressive.

What the Trust would do now

The Trust would adopt the legal 'tramlines' or a standard contract which should help simplify the contract negotiations and reduce legal expenses as well as the length of the procurement process.

The Trust would pay greater attention to affordability earlier and from the outset of the project. It would have made greater efforts to factor in the full costs of risks into the cost of the public sector comparator which was identified at the OBC stage.

It would evaluate the consortium's strength in greater depth to try to assess what their commitment to closing the deal was like and what 'back up' they had if key people left.

It would insist on more detailed design at a much earlier stage: there is no doubt that banks will only lend against clearly defined prospective assets (i.e. detailed 1:50 drawings, which doctors as well as the Trust have signed off).

Consistency with lessons from other schemes

These lessons are consistent with what is known about other capital schemes in the health sector. Writing about the experience of the Mayday NHS Trust's power generation and waste products project, John Corlett, director of facilities, noted a number of additional lessons, most notably the need:

- for feasibility studies to be realistic and not fudged to produce the desired results
- to research the market well and find out what is going on elsewhere in both the private and public sectors
- to employ experienced advisers with a proven track record in advising on PFI procurements
- to remember that PFI projects are fundamentally about provision of services, hence the need for the public sector clients to resist the temptation of getting bogged down over the technical aspects of the scheme
- to produce 'fit for purpose' OBSs which produce a clear steer to the private sector about the desired quantity and quality of services
- to obtain clarification from the preferred partner on all the key criteria laid down in the ITT as soon as possible and not to be afraid of pulling the plug if the goal posts have changed. 'It may cost in abortive time and fees, but is much less painful in the long run. Remember, it is not always the best sales presentation that delivers the best product'
- for the lead member of the consortium to adopt an entrepreneurial role. 'Don't negotiate with a committee – keep communication links as short as possible, including within the client organisation'
- to ensure there is a good audit trail covering all aspects of the procurement (Davidson 1998).

The last point is significant. Like death, it is a certainty that the public and watchdog bodies like the NAO will review how public sector bodies conduct the procurement and the robustness of the decision-making process. The project documents will provide a key source of evidence to such investigations. It is important for future procurements to learn from the experience of pathfinder schemes. The former are expected to demonstrate an improvement on the latter, particularly in the areas of value for money, contract terms, affordability and fees paid to advisers.

CHAPTER EIGHT

Case study 2: PFI procurement of information technology services

This chapter provides a case study on the procurement of information services and technology (IS/IT), based on the experience of Liverpool Women's Hospital. This was the first IS/IT project to be privately financed in the NHS. Written largely by David Young, Director of Finance, the chapter discusses the planning and execution of the project from establishing the business need to the commencement of services. Emphasis is placed on generic lessons to guide future procurements. The lessons are particularly relevant to delivering the strategic requirements of the DoH's pathbreaking information strategy, *Information for Health*, launched in September 1998.

Introduction

Liverpool Women's Hospital was planned and built in the early 1990s, finally opening to its first patients in February 1995. Construction of the hospital, which predated the PFI, had progressed through a design and build process. Part of that project included the infrastructure to enable hospital-wide information systems to be installed. At the time of opening a contract for the provision of information services was nearing its conclusion. The information and IT strategy that had been produced within the Trust indicated that the installation of a full Hospital Information Support System (HISS) through a facilities management contract was the preferred route for meeting future information needs. The drawing up of the specification for this new system coincided with the introduction of PFI in the NHS. As a result, the specification, procurement, contract and business planning for the HISS progressed through the PFI process. The scheme became the first approved PFI procurement for information services in the NHS in England.

Following approval to proceed in February 1996, final negotiations were undertaken with prospective suppliers leading to the award of the contract in April 1996. Renegotiation of some contract terms due to a change in project finance meant that contracts for the HISS were not signed until July 1996. Implementation work had already begun at this time, enabling the initial modules of the new system to go live on 9 December 1996. These replicated the pre-existing patient administration system and some clinical functionality. Subsequent to going live, further modules have been implemented giving additional clinical functionality. The development of all functionality specified in the PFI contract is likely to continue until the end of 1999/2000 when a level 3 HISS will have been achieved.

Background to the Trust

Prior to the 1990 NHS reorganisation, health services in Liverpool were administered through a number of directly managed units under the auspices of Liverpool Health Authority. Those services providing care for women and babies were organised under an obstetrics and gynaecology unit. Services were provided from three hospitals: Mill Road Maternity Hospital, Liverpool Maternity Hospital and the Women's Hospital, Catherine Street. In addition, two wards at the Royal Liverpool University Hospital were also involved in provision of gynaecology and assisted reproduction.

On 1 April 1992, the Liverpool Obstetrics and Gynaecology Services NHS Trust was formed to manage services for women and babies. Plans were in hand at this time for the establishment of a new hospital to replace the existing buildings. The planning for this hospital had commenced in 1990 with a view to a new hospital opening in summer 1994. A number of planning difficulties were encountered that postponed the planned opening date until February 1995. In the early 1990s a number of rationalisation steps were taken towards the merger of the old hospitals into the new building. These were successfully concluded early in 1995 when services were moved into the new

Liverpool Women's Hospital which opened formally for its first patients in February of that year.

Information services in the Trust

Following a procurement exercise, Liverpool Health Authority signed contracts to install computerised information systems commencing in 1989. These services were to cover all acute hospitals within its remit. In all, ten hospitals were involved in the project (subsequently becoming five separate Trusts) and an extended implementation period was inevitable. The women's hospitals installed a partial HISS in 1991 as part of this contract with SMS (UK) Ltd which was due to run to 30 June 1996. Under the contract the hospitals were supplied with terminals linked via local and wide area networks (LANs and WANs) in Warrington where the central processing hardware was located. The provision of all facilities management services was managed by IT Services as subcontractor to SMS.

As a result of this service supply arrangement there was only a small IT department within the hospital. This comprised the HISS project manager, two training/helpdesk staff and one technician under the control of the Head of Information and Patient Services. The hospitals had no direct involvement in the management of IT equipment other than day-to-day support of terminal users and maintenance of a small office network of personal computers used by the management team.

The services provided in the Women's Hospital comprised the following applications:

- admissions
- out-patient scheduling
- waiting list
- contract management
- nurse care planning
- order entry
- end user reporting
- maternity.

All the applications were integrated products except the maternity module from EIT which was standalone with a duplex interface to the SMS admissions and out-patient applications.

The development of the interface from SMS to EIT took over two years to complete and, when implemented, required significant day-to-day attention to maintain service between the two systems. The user interfaces of the products from the two suppliers were very different, one purely character-based and the other offering a mix of character-based and bar-coded data entry. Screen layouts and the use of functions key also differed between the two systems.

Extent of the implementation

All admissions, transfers and discharges were recorded on the SMS admissions module. All recording took place on the relevant ward; out-patient clinics were managed via the SMS out-patient module; waiting lists were administered via the SMS waiting list module; patients admitted to the gynaecology wards were allocated a nursing care plan via the SMS care-planning module; contracts (purchaser/provider) managed through the SMS contract management module; antenatal booking visits and deliveries recorded on the EIT maternity system; and district nursing, dietetic and Macmillian nursing requests from gynae-cology wards processed through the SMS order entry module.

The Trust's IM&T strategy

As part of the work in preparation for the move to the new hospital and the replacement of its existing information systems, the Trust undertook a review of its information and IT strategy during 1994. This exercise took into account the views of all major staff groups, particularly consultants and clinical professionals. At that time the ability to provide management information to inform the contract-ing and business planning processes was the main focus of the systems.

The strategy developed by the Trust identified management needs as the most immediate requirement, but acknowledged that the future of information services would centre on better clinical information. The main objectives of the strategy were:

- more effective activity monitoring and better information for budgetary control and staff time deployment
- more meaningful case categorisation to enable better comparative clinical review, better defined contracts and more accurate pricing
- use of information to demonstrate the quality of the service provided, hence generating increased contractual income
- reduced repetitive recording of data items and reduced need for cross-checking of data and information
- enabling better management of the skill mix of staff.

It was expected that patient care would be improved through achieving these objectives. This was to be achieved through an indirect process of audit and education rather than as a direct result of the use of information systems in the clinical areas.

The strategy discussed the relative merits of the various system architectures that were then available and concluded that a fully integrated HISS, provided under a facilities management contract by a lead contractor, would best meet the present and future needs of the Trust. The main components of the HISS identified in the strategy were:

- patient administration system
- maternity system
- ward ordering and results reporting
- theatre system
- contract management system
- radiology system
- pharmacy system
- nursing system
- clinical audit systems.

An outline timetable for the introduction of the new systems was included in the strategy. This envisaged a single go-live date for all replacement and new applications to coincide with the end date of the existing contract with SMS.

Within the strategy a number of options for procurement of the systems were discussed and evaluated, the most favoured option being the continuation of a facilities management arrangement. As the Trust was already operating under this type of contract there were no concerns about the potential loss of assets or the control of those assets. On the contrary, the plans for the new hospital (then under construction) expressly excluded facilities for any information or IT presence. There was no space allocated for computer rooms or for the associated staffing. The plans included the basic communications infrastructure built around a fibre optic backbone connecting three communications rooms serving all parts of the hospital via a conventional wired network.

IM&T organisation

Throughout the project the Trust used the PRINCE project management methodology with the Trust IM&T Steering Board acting as the top level project board (*see* Box 8.1).

Box 8.1: IM&T Steering Board

Chief Executive Officer (Executive)
Director of Finance (senior technical)
Medical Director
Non-executive Director
Director of Nursing and Midwifery (senior user)
Head of Information and Patient Services (project manager)
Head of Information Technology

HISS implementation project board
Head of Information and Patient Services (system owner Patient Administration)
Head of Information Technology (project manager)
Director of Finance (chairperson)
Senior Pharmacy Technician (system owner Pharmacy)
Project Ultrasonographer (system owner Radiology)
Theatre Manager (system owner Theatres)
Ward Manager (system owner Care planning/Order entry)
Clinical consultant (System owner Medical Systems)
Obstetrics Manager (system owner Maternity)
Deputy Director of Finance (system owner Materials Management)

The IM&T Steering Board met on a quarterly basis or as required throughout the entire period of the project, from strategy formulation through procurement to implementation. It is anticipated that this will continue through the review of the systems implementation and formulation of the next generation IS/IT strategy. While the posts involved are fixed, membership is dynamic and the present Board has no member who was in post at the start of the project.

Reporting to this board is the HISS implementation project board comprising of the project manager and a group of senior managers from departments and directorates who have taken responsibility for individual HISS modules (the system owner). The HISS project board meets on a bi-weekly basis or as required.

Management of the Trust's IM&T organisation is closely aligned to that of the IM&T strategy and the Trust's business plan. The IM&T Steering Board reviews the IM&T organisation on a quarterly basis to ensure clarity, consistency and coverage of the necessary roles and responsibilities.

The investment decision

Needs identification

A detailed statement of need (DSON) was developed by the Trust during the summer of 1994. A number of system owners were tasked with identifying the detailed requirements for their particular work areas. These requirements were reviewed by the HISS project board and drawn together into the DSON.

The DSON was subsequently refined to produce an output-based summary of need (SON) that was issued to suppliers. The DSON and SON were subsequently included as appendices 1 and 4 in the Schedules to Contract with the successful tenderer, Data General (UK) Ltd.

Option generation

The Trust's IM&T Strategy (1994) proposed that the preferred direction for the Trust would be:

> An integrated HISS product (using one product supplied by one supplier) covering the majority of clinically related service functions. This would minimise duplicate data entry, make information more freely available through the Trust and the system would be more easily maintained and supported. Inevitably, systems such as finance, supplies and personnel would probably remain outside the integrated product, but the

number of necessary 'interworking' solutions required would be radically reduced.

There was, however, a range of options which would have enabled the Trust to fulfil its information requirements in terms of outputs required for patient administration, billing and (with varying degrees of functionality) enabling improvement in patient care. These existed on a continuum, with varying degrees of computerisation from purely manual systems to full integration of all systems in one IT solution.

For the purposes of evaluation a number of points on the continuum were selected, each one representing a clear stage in the transition to a fully integrated solution, as follows:

1 Reversion to full manual systems.
2 Continuation of existing mix of computerised and manual systems (partial HISS) – the 'do nothing' option.
3 Increase HISS functionality to cover those systems considered as core systems in the Trust's IM&T strategy.
4 Extend functionality to a full HISS to include clinical departmental systems but excluding non-clinical systems such as finance, personnel and supplies.
5 A fully integrated total information system, including all patient administration and clinical areas plus finance, personnel and supplies.

Option 1 – revert to manual systems

Although a partial HISS had been in place in the Trust for four years there were still a number of manual systems in operation. It would have been possible, given suitable investment in human resources, to revert to manual systems for data capture and information processing across the full range of the Trust's information systems.

To have proceeded in this way would have been contrary to the Trust's business and IM&T strategies, and additionally would not have been in line with the then NHS IM&T strategy – *Getting Better with Information*. It would have caused significant disruption to the clinical, administrative and business processes and could have resulted in the Trust failing to achieve key clinical and business goals.

The Trust had gained significant benefits through its previous IT implementations which would have been lost or reduced if manual systems were imposed. These disbenefits included:

- additional staffing for medical records, secretarial services, contracting and billing, information processing and clinical audit
- multiple data recording, with the danger of differences in data between parallel databases, and time spent cross-checking
- loss of timeliness in providing information, leading to delays in implementation of corrective action
- delays in billing leading to potential loss of contract income, particularly with regard to extra-contractual referrals (ECRs) and GP fundholders
- reduction in quality of out-patient administration, affecting the efficiency of the department, clarity of correspondence and achievement of Patient's Charter standards
- reduction in quality of maternity notes, leading to poorer case management and increased pressure on midwifery time
- ultimate loss of competitive positioning.

Overall this option was not considered viable, but was evaluated as it represented a baseline position from which benefits had already been achieved.

Option 2 – 'do nothing – continue with existing systems'

The Trust identified its 'do nothing' option as negotiating a new contract with the current supplier to supply the existing level of service to the Trust. This service comprised a facilities management contract for:

- patient administration system
- maternity system
- nursing system
- ward ordering and results reporting
- end user reporting
- accident and emergency systems
- contracting system
- systems operation and network services.

This option had a number of intrinsic advantages in that it represented a continuation of existing systems. As staff were already trained and experienced, there would be no disruption caused by change to systems or methods of work.

There were, however, significant disadvantages compared with other options which provided extended functionality. These included:

- failure to deliver any additional benefits beyond those already available
- limited functionality of ward ordering and results reporting due to the lack of linkages with feeder systems such as theatres, pathology, radiology, etc.
- increasing maintenance/support costs notified by the supplier above current levels
- the Trust would wish to make a thorough market review at the end of ten years.

Option 3 – 'core systems'

Option 3 was to negotiate a contract for 'core systems' as defined in the Trust's IM&T strategy:

- patient administration system
- maternity system
- nursing system
- ward ordering and results reporting
- audit
- theatre system
- accident and emergency systems
- contracting system
- end user reporting.

This represented an extension of the functionality detailed in Option 2.

This option provided a number of additional benefits to those being achieved, resulting from improved ward ordering and results reporting through linkages with the theatre and pharmacy systems. The availability of integrated audit and improved end user reporting would facilitate better clinical management.

The core systems did not include pharmacy, pathology or radiology, so benefits would have been limited in those areas. This option also required some changes in working practices in order to achieve the extensions in functionality listed. These would be minimal if an extension of the existing suppliers systems were used, but if a new supplier was selected there would be substantial changes required, though without the paybacks of the full package of benefits anticipated from options with greater functionality.

Option 4 – full HISS

Option 4 was to replace or develop the Trust's existing systems to a full HISS. This would include departmental systems, which would be fully linked or integrated to provide an information base with minimal duplication of input and maximum flexibility for retrieval of clinical and other data.

The systems included in this option were:

- patient administration system
- maternity system
- nursing system
- ward ordering and results reporting
- audit
- theatre system
- accident and emergency systems
- contracting system
- end user reporting
- radiology
- pharmacy
- GP links
- interface to pathology and neonatal systems.

This option maximised the availability of benefits flowing from the integration of clinical information systems, and also included the facility to link with GPs for exchanging clinical correspondence, reports and booking of patient appointments.

To achieve these benefits there would be a number of significant changes to methods of working, particularly if the supplier changed and, consequently, new software systems were adopted. These changes in practice extended across all areas where the systems were in place and were critical, given the limited timescales envisaged for implementation.

Option 5 – total integrated systems

This option included all the clinical areas set out for Option 4, but additionally included integrated financial, manpower and purchasing systems to deliver a single system to cover all the Trust's information and data handling requirements.

In considering the practical implications of this option, the following factors emerged:

- the Trust's IM&T strategy considered such an option but rejected it in favour of concentrating on an integrated HISS with functional linkages to the non-clinical systems
- the initial scan of the market did not reveal any systems which offer a fully integrated and acceptable solution across all functional areas
- any bespoke development would be beyond the managerial and technical manpower resources of the Trust and would introduce elements of risk which would be unacceptable
- the existing balance of integrating clinical systems, with separate financial, payroll, personnel and purchasing systems, was operating satisfactorily
- changing all the Trust's systems at one time in the absence of a demonstrably proven single solution was not considered practicable or desirable when weighed against the potential risks involved.

For these reasons this option was not considered in any detail and was eliminated at the shortlisting stage.

In the event that the system ultimately selected had the additional functionality to provide financial, manpower or purchasing systems, the Trust would consider the development of its use, but these areas were not evaluated as part of the HISS procurement.

Review of available solutions

In the period between development of the IS/IT strategy and the procurement of the replacement HISS, great emphasis was put on the comprehensive review of systems available in the market at that time. Informal visits were made to HISS sites around the country to learn from their teams about the ways in which their projects had been organised and the benefits arising from the individual local solutions they had adopted.

These visits included consultant medical staff and senior clinical professionals as well as the IT and information specialists. This approach was as much to inform the participants of the potential uses of information in the clinical environment as to assess the capabilities of the proprietary systems themselves. In addition the visits, which often required overnight stays, were helpful in building the multi-disciplinary teams which would become fundamental to the successful implementation that was ultimately to follow.

Among the sites visited were:

- Queen's Hospital, Burton on Trent
- City Hospital, Sunderland
- Arrowe Park Hospital, Wirral
- Queen Elizabeth Hospital, Birmingham
- Greenwich District Hospital, London
- Ipswich Hospital.

Visits were also made by the multidisciplinary groups to the premises of a number of system suppliers to review prototype and developmental systems demonstrations.

Business case development

In line with the capital expenditure procedures, the business case for the HISS replacement was formulated in two separate stages: OBC and FBC.

Outline Business Case

The development of the OBC took place in the period September to December 1994. The development of the document was complicated by the requirement that the NHS should participate in the PFI. This resulted in the need to develop a strategic context document to accompany a more comprehensive OBC. The documents covered the following areas:

- strategic context
- definition of objectives and benefit criteria
- option generation
- measurement of benefits
- identification and quantification of associated costs
- assessment of sensitivity to risk
- identification of the preferred option.

Option 4 was identified as the preferred option in both the financial and non-financial analyses. Option 4 met all the desired benefits identified in the strategy. With appropriate risk management it was considered that this option would function effectively and would be affordable on the basis of costing information available at the time.

The process of document development was managed through a subgroup of the HISS Procurement Board. This group comprised:

- Head of IM&T
- procurement project manager
- deputy project manager
- deputy Director of Finance
- specialty manager for neonatology.

Full Business Case

The FBC presented the case for the procurement of a hospital-wide information system. The preferred option identified in the OBC was to procure systems covering the full operational scope of the Trust, with the exception of personnel, payroll and financial systems. This represented an extension of the systems used at that time in the Trust.

A wide range of benefits to patients, GPs and to the Trust were identified that would result from the procurement and implementation of appropriate systems. These benefits would:

- improve patient satisfaction
- improve patient administration
- improve planning and resource utilisation
- enhance the clinical quality of care
- improve staff satisfaction
- gain a competitive advantage for the Trust.

A thorough benefits identification exercise was undertaken, and a realisation plan drawn up.

The business case reviewed the technical options available to the Trust and considered alternative financing arrangements. The technical option remained unchanged from the OBC because of the wide range of additional benefits that would accrue under this option.

In financing terms, the Trust received a number of proposals under the PFI, and these proposals were compared with the publicly funded options. The PFI proposals included a range of contractual features that would shift risk from the Trust and to the supplier.

When examined in terms of risk transfer and the benefits that would be accrued from the proposals, the net result of the contractual arrangements was that the PFI options would cost less than the best available PSC. In its negotiations with suppliers, the Trust agreed a framework for:

- payment drivers
- incentives

- a service level agreement
- other contractual terms and conditions.

Following full evaluation and comparison of the supplier's proposals against the technical requirements, the preferred option was to enter a PFI contract with Data General to provide the Meditech HISS system. The full life (seven years) cost of the project was £3.7m.

Role of advisers

Document development for the FBC was managed by a small group of Trust personnel: Director of Finance, Head of IM&T and procurement project manager. Consideration was given to the use of outside consultants to assist in the production of the FBC. This was dismissed because: PFI knowledge was not generally available in the NHS context; there had been no PFI approvals from which to gain any lessons or comfort; and no consultancy firm could demonstrate any better knowledge than that available in-house. The business case was also regarded as an integral part of the cultural development of the organisation. As such, to hand it over to an outsider would be to rob the Trust of the collective experience of putting together its future plans. Finances were limited and clinical spending took a higher priority.

In order to meet a perceived need for NHS Supplies' advice, their assistance was sought and a contract entered into for procurement support and contractual advice. At the time the NHS Supplies organisation was not organised to give effective advice on PFI contracts, resulting in the use of the in-house purchasing department to advise on procurement rules and to undertake the necessary supplier evaluations prior to tendering. Heavy use was made of the Trust's lawyers, Hill Dickinson Davis Campbell, who drew up the draft contracts, advised on their commercial content and helped with the negotiations with potential suppliers.

The expertise of the partner assigned to the project and her ability to quickly assimilate the requirements of the PFI were invaluable and became imperative to the project in the difficult period between award of tender and the final signing of the contract. This was made more difficult because the Data General legal department was based in the United States and time differences intruded on the contract negotiations.

Approval process for OBC

The approval process for both the OBC and FBC posed a number of problems for the Trust. During the development of the OBC the HISS central team informed the Trust that a new initiative was coming into play: PFI. This required a more output-based approach to the business case with a much more rigorous approach to risk identification and allocation. In addition, there was now a requirement to develop a Strategic Context document. The decision was made by the Trust to revise the documents to reflect the incoming initiative. This introduced a delay in producing them. The dates for the development and submission of the OBC and Strategic Context are detailed in Appendix A.

The OBC was first submitted to the Trust's main purchaser for their approval. The Regional Office was then involved and approval to proceed was subsequently granted. This approval was given on the basis that the investment should result in no upwards effect on contract prices to purchasers, and should ideally be financed via the PFI.

Procurement process

Following approval of the OBC, attempts were made to place an advertisement in the OJEC. Owing to problems in wording to include the UK PFI, the first advertisement was deemed to be invalid and a second advertisement was required. This advertisement was placed in February 1995, asking for expressions of interest in supplying a replacement hospital administration system. It resulted in 35 responses, ranging in capability from a local business supplying mouse mats and computer stationery to a number of multinational corporations.

The SON was issued to 16 firms together with a number of documents asking for a range of technical and business information to assist in the shortlisting process: pre-qualification questionnaire; NHS STEP questionnaire; response to the Trust's output-based Summary of Need; and five-year financial results.

Replies were received from five companies. A panel comprising members of the HISS project board, assisted by NHS Supplies, reviewed these responses in detail together with independent credit ratings and financial enquiries. The criteria used were:

- performance against mandatory requirements outlined in the summary of need

- performance against STEP questionnaire; cost; company policy with regard to PFI
- ability to meet proposed timescales
- supplier's strategic development proposals
- performance against non-mandatory requirements outlined in the SON
- assessment of working relationships
- credit rating
- experience of working under a facilities management contract.

From the five responses, three companies were shortlisted. These included the incumbent system supplier plus the two best bids as submitted. It would have been possible to include a fourth company but it was considered that the additional choice available was outweighed by the additional work involved in maintaining a longer shortlist.

At the time of shortlisting, the PFI rules precluded a single supplier shortlist. A shorter list was considered but dismissed. It was considered essential to maintain two other options in addition to the incumbent supplier to prevent a single supplier shortlist in the event of a withdrawal at later stages of procurement. The final shortlist was announced on 1 August 1995.

Full Business Case

The FBC was developed during the summer/autumn of 1995, in parallel with the shortlisting of potential suppliers.

The approval process involved the following stages:

- Submission to Liverpool Health Authority, the Trust's main purchaser, in September 1995. Their approval criteria had not changed since the OBC submission and consequently the FBC was given full approval within one week.
- Submission to the Regional Office in October 1995. Staff at the Regional Office had little previous experience of IT business case evaluation under PFI and consequently sought external help in order to turn the case round quickly. Early in November a response was received asking for a significant number of changes and expansion of a number of points in the FBC. The main issues raised related to the analysis of risk, the strategic context and some technical issues in

the discounted cash-flow calculations. These points were dealt with in an appendix to the FBC.
- Submission to NHS Executive headquarters in December 1995. Following reconsideration by the Regional Office, formal approval to submit the case to the NHS Executive in Leeds was received at the end of November 1995.

In parallel with submission to the Regional Office, a draft copy of the FBC was sent informally to the NHS Executive in Leeds for perusal by the Information Management Group and the Capital Investment Unit. Contact had been made with these officials at a very early stage to seek guidance and advice on the expectations of the new system. As there was considerable interest in the Liverpool Women's Hospital case, the opportunity was taken at every stage to seek informal comments and guidance to improve the content and presentation of the FBC.

Initial evaluation in Leeds was carried out quickly and further information and clarification was requested. The areas requiring further elucidation were:

- linkages between the Trust's objectives, its IM&T strategy and the proposed investment
- clarification of the options used in the appraisal
- consideration of best of breed solutions as well as the integrated solutions identified
- confirmation that the benefits identified were realistic and that each had a named person responsible for its delivery
- clarification of the project management arrangements and responsibilities
- further clarification and quantification of risks associated with the project
- confirmation that the preferred PFI option had a lower net present cost than the public sector comparator before taking risk into consideration.

All these issues were addressed in a further appendix to the FBC that was sent to the NHS Executive in mid-December 1995. This was accepted and forwarded to HM Treasury for final approval.

Approval to the FBC was initially refused due to the perceived lack of a clear financial benefit from the PFI purchase in comparison with the capital purchase alternative.

Failure to gain approval to the business case was a severe blow to the Trust and in particular to the team who had been working on the document. There were also immediate financial consequences of failure: it was clear that there was no possibility of implementation of any replacement system before the end of the existing facilities management contract. Negotiations had been taking place throughout the reprocurement with the incumbent supplier to extend the existing contract in the event of the FBC not gaining approval.

Options were available to extend for six months at a small premium on top of the contract rate or for a full year at a much higher premium. The increased costs were due to the urgent need to replace some items of hardware and software in order to maintain continuity of service. As there was still some residual confidence that the FBC would eventually be approved, the decision to extend for six months was taken which put back the 'drop dead date' for any new system implementation to 31 December 1995.

In January 1996, all parties to the FBC approval were lobbied in order to try to clear the impasse that had emerged. After a number of extended and fruitless conversations with individual parties to the approval process it was agreed that, as a last resort, a meeting of all parties would be held at the NHS Executive headquarters to attempt to break the deadlock. It was clear that there was considerable pressure to reach a positive outcome to the meeting. From the Trust's perspective the financial arguments in favour of the preferred PFI solution were irrefutable. For the NHS Executive and Treasury there was an urgent need to gain the confidence of the NHS and the IT industry that PFI solutions to IT problems in the NHS could be found.

After considerable negotiation at which further clarification was presented, together with some minor improvements that had been agreed with potential suppliers, a way ahead was agreed. The necessary amendment to the business case was made the following day and submitted to all parties. Conditional approval to proceed was granted on 29 February 1996.

Tendering and contracts

In the period when the FBC was being considered, one of the three shortlisted suppliers took the decision to withdraw from the project. This was due to their strategic decision to concentrate their marketing effort in other markets where procurement processes were not so protracted as in the NHS in England. The two remaining suppliers were invited to tender in March 1996 on the basis of the specifications that had been agreed during the pre-tender period. Contract terms had been discussed in general terms though the fine detail of payment drivers and any proposals for transfer payments at the end of the contract were left open to the tender stage.

Receipt of the tenders confirmed Data General as the cheaper provider. This applied in terms of the tender price and also attitude to PFI with a bid that included acceptable levels of risk transfer through the payment drivers and a significant transfer payment proposal. As a consequence, Data General was appointed as PFI partner in April 1995.

There followed a period of post-tender negotiation, principally around risk transfer, which delayed the signing of the contract. Unfortunately the bank that had agreed to fund the project withdrew because of perceived risks with PFI payment streams in the event of the NHS Trust's financial failure. At the time, the government would not guarantee PFI contracts and the bank would settle for nothing less than a cast-iron guarantee from the Secretary of State. Over a period of two months Data General were forced to find new financial support for PFI projects. A Belgian bank was willing to fund such projects and negotiations between them and Data General were speedily completed, subject to changes to the contract with Liverpool Women's Hospital. The changes involving contract termination and step-in rights in the event of failure to provide services to the required quality were difficult and protracted but finally agreement was reached and contracts were executed in July 1996.

Contract terms

The contract term is for seven years and full details of the terms and conditions can be found in the Schedules to Contract, Schedule appendices and Terms and Conditions. The principal PFI contract terms relate to the payment of the contract sum and the sharing of risk. As originally constructed, the delivery and implementation of the HISS was scheduled in three phases over a 12-month period. Each phase attached a proportion of the total contract sum payable on acceptance of the phase by the Trust. Conditions in the contract allowed retention of a proportion of the phase payment if implementation was delayed beyond agreed time-limits by the contractor.

The structure of payments due to Data General is set out in schedule G of the contract. The main elements of this are:

- 70% of payment for the phase payable on acceptance and annually thereafter
- 30% of payment for the phase payable quarterly in arrears, dependent

on meeting agreed performance levels. Within this payment the performance drivers shown in Table 8.1 are used.

During the course of the first two phases of the contract it was agreed that the presence of a payment driver linked to system usage was inappropriate due to the developing nature of the functionality. The payment driver measures usage by a clinical cohort, though the clinical functionality is not fully present until the final implementation of the third phase. At that stage the most pressing need from the Trust's point of view was the implementation of developments and tailoring of the systems to meet the needs set out in schedule J. It was agreed that in order to give incentive and reward for delivery of the changes, including a number that had not become apparent until the implementation was well advanced, the usage payment driver be postponed for two periods and the available funding transferred to the minor software changes category. This change worked well in practice, resulting in timely delivery of the changes required to the system.

Table 8.1: Performance drivers

Type of payment driver	Payment driver	% of annual contract value
System performance and availability	Help desk response times	3%
	System availability	4%
	System response times	3%
Usage	Usage	10%
Cost of change	Statutory changes	4%
	General upgrades	3%
	Minor software changes	3%
Total		30%

Risk assessment

One of the critical factors in the business case was the identification, valuation and management of risk. The potential risks to the project were identified and assessed by the project team using a variety of sources for ideas and experience. Table 8.2 sets out the key risks and indicates the risk-sharing methodology proposed by the Trust to deal with them.

Table 8.2: Key risks and proposed risk-sharing methodology

Identified risk element	Strategy	Comments
Systems not delivered on time	Penalty on supplier for each module where delivery is late	Fixed penalty for modules which replace existing, e.g. Patient Master Index, penalty related to benefits lost for new modules, e.g. theatre
Third party software not delivered on time	Responsibility of prime contractor	Penalty in contract terms for non-delivery of outputs
Software developments not implemented to agreed timescale	Supplier to meet costs of maintaining existing systems	Risk variable for suppliers dependent on the number of new products offered (also see below)
Software developments fail to meet specification	No payment to supplier and additional costs (if any) passed on to supplier	Option of sharing benefits to supplier of new software to be explored, e.g. development of maternity system has potential as a market leader for widespread sales in the NHS
Training not delivered to agreed timescale	Penalty on supplier	Variable penalty linked to slippage against training plan
Staff not available to be trained	Task to be included in managers' objectives	Trust to bear risk
Loss of key staff, such as project manager or system owners	Additional staff to be trained to shadow key responsibilities	Residual risk of loss of momentum to be borne by the Trust Possibility of support by supplier to be explored
Delay in business case submission and/or approval	Ensure timescales are met and communication with the centre maintained	High degree of uncertainty about success criteria

Identified risk element	Strategy	Comments
Unrealistic implementation plan	Agree with supplier and Trust staff responsible for implementation	Agreement will enable sharing of risk, with phasing to minimise total risk exposure
Supplier goes out of business	Shortlisted suppliers subjected to financial scrutiny and reviewed to ensure continued stability	Financial guarantees and/or performance bonds to be sought in contract negotiation without additional cost to the Trust
Benefits not delivered due to system implementation/ delivery/quality problems	Benefits realisation plan to be agreed with supplier. Penalty on supplier for their failure	Penalty equal to loss of benefits due to supplier's failure
Benefits not delivered due to Trust failure to manage	Implementation and benefits realisation to be part of managers' objectives	Lost benefits to be borne by Trust
Quality of outputs falls below specification	Supplier to meet cost of reaching specified output quality	Additional penalty if timescales also over-run
Hardware becomes obsolescent or fails to deliver response/quality required to maintain software outputs	Supplier to be responsible for refreshment of hardware at no additional cost within contract	Unlikely to be achievable with capital purchase options
Hardware wrongly sized to deliver outputs specified	Upgrade at supplier's cost, including any associated licences	
Ownership problems, such as physical security, data security	Offsite facilities management contract	Minimises some risks but equipment still present on site will require security strategy
Implementation costs exceed budget	Negotiate fixed price with supplier	Could include sharing of savings if costs, e.g. of training, are below budget due to Trust actions

Table 8.2: (*cont.*)

Identified risk element	Strategy	Comments
Service disruption due to unfamiliarity with new systems	Training plan to be structured to prevent this occurring	Loss due to supplier failure to be passed on as penalty Loss due to Trust failure to manage borne by Trust
Output requirements change due to local or central government action	Supplier to be encouraged to provide flexible software and to bear costs of centrally required change	Trust to bear cost of specific tailoring after reasonable bedding-in period, say 2–3 years
Changes in the volume of core business, i.e. current activities	Potential for thresholds in facilities management contract to be explored with suppliers	
Changes to the range of business require changes to functionality	Software flexibility to be negotiated into contract	Expect that additional modules would be at cost to the Trust, but extension of modules in use would be responsibility of supplier
Trust involved in merger with other provider(s)	Procure open systems	Merging of information systems likely to be a major problem unless all parties coming from the same base
Operational response falls below acceptable levels	Agree service levels and incorporate acceptable performance measures as a payment driver	Applies to response times, help-desk services, system availability, etc.

Change control within the contract

Schedule H of the Schedules to Contract for the Managed Service defines the process for the management of change to the contract during its term. If the Trust or the prime contractor sees the need for change to functionality, system interfaces, inputs, outputs, project timescales or to the way that the service is implemented and provided, the Trust may at any time request and the contractor may at any time recommend such changes and propose an amendment to the contract in accordance with the formal Change Control Procedure (CCP) as set out in schedule H.

The Trust and the contractor discuss changes proposed by either party and such discussion results in agreement not to proceed further, a written request for a change by the Trust, or a recommendation for a change by the contractor.

Each Change Control Notice (CCN) contains:

- the title of the change
- the originator and date of the request or recommendation for the change
- the reason for the change
- the full details of the change, including any specifications and user facilities
- the price, if any, of the change
- a timetable for implementation together with any proposals for acceptance of the change
- a schedule of payments if appropriate
- the impact, if any, of the change on other aspects of the contract including:
  - milestone
  - the overall contractual timetable
  - the project implementation plan
  - the contract price/contract charges
  - the overall payment schedule
  - documentation lists
  - resources
  - contractual issues
  - serviceability and performance levels
  - system configuration, including store utilisation
  - throughput
  - resilience

- the date for expiry of validity of the CCN
- provision for signature by the Trust and the contractor.

Problem management

The contractor provides help-desk facilities 24 hours a day, 365 days a year for major and critical incidents. For software and hardware activities required to maintain and update the service, the contractor is required to programme activities so that they do not affect services during the hours of 8am to 6pm, Monday to Friday. Outside these hours, the contractor provides a point of contact who is able to diagnose the type of problem and direct remedial action by the Trust and the contractor.

Security and back-up recovery

The contractor ensures that the system hardware is kept in a physically secure environment.

All data are backed up by the contractor once every 24 hours at least and a copy of the backed-up data is moved by the contractor to a separate site from the managed service on a daily basis.

The contractor also undertakes to provide full system back-ups on a regular basis and they too are stored by the contractor on a separate site from the managed service. Both the system hardware and data back-ups are maintained in a fireproof, physically secure, access-controlled environment that is also isolated from variations in power supply. In the event of the disaster recovery procedure being invoked, data recovery will take place according to the procedure in Appendix 13 of the Schedules to Contract.

Options at the end of the contract

The Trust has the option under the schedules to the contract with Data General Ltd to automatically extend the term of the contract to a maximum of three years beyond the initial termination of date. There is an automatic termination to the contract after the expiry of three years from the end of the initial term. The term of the extension will in practice be governed by any EEC regulation/best NHS practice guidance that is applicable.

Payment under the extension provisions is covered in the schedule where a formula is set out indicating the proportion of the contract sum that is payable for each of the quarters beyond the initial termination date. This formula reflects the ongoing benefit to the Trust for the use of the system and also the reduced cost to the contractor once the initial contract period is completed. During this extension period all performance criteria apply as in the initial term, though the withholding of the proportion of the payment due as a transfer payment does not apply.

Should the Trust decide not to extend the contract under the automatic provisions then formal reprocurement would follow. This action would also be required at the end of any extension period as described above. Reprocurement would follow the format required under the NHS procurement regulations applicable at that time.

In the event of Data General being successful in winning the new contract, the transfer payment withheld during the term of the initial contract would be payable to them as reward for their performance. In the event of another contractor winning the contract the transfer payment would be used to defray the costs of reprocurement.

Provision also exists within the contract for the continued use of the system at the end of the term, but with a new service provider. If this provision were brought into play then either the Trust or the new contractor is required to pay to Data General a sum equivalent to the transfer payment as consideration for the transfer of title to the hardware and access to the software.

Accounting treatment for the HISS contract

The contract between Liverpool Women's Hospital and Data General Ltd is clearly defined as a facilities management arrangement. The Trust has no access under the contract to any equipment or building other than as a result of the application of the termination arrangements for failure to deliver services to the required specification.

Advice was sought from the Trust's auditors on the correct accounting treatment, given that there were no assets accessible to the Trust. It was agreed that a continuation of the previous accounting treatment for a non-PFI-managed service agreement would be appropriate. In accordance with this, annual payments to the contractor are accounted for through the income and expenditure statement and there is no impact on the balance sheet. This is in line with the guidance in FRS5 and SSAP22.

Lessons from the procurement and implementation

1 Allow ample time for planning and procurement

It is clear from the timetables from the procurement and implementation set out in Appendix A that a period of at least two years should be allowed for PFI procurement from the point of agreeing a strategy to the date of implementation. This is a minimum requirement from experience of a relatively straightforward procurement that received priority at all stages in its existence.

Appropriate time should be made available at all stages with suitable allowances for:

- preparation of the overall IS/IT strategy
- review of systems available in the marketplace
- preparation of the OBC and FBC
- negotiation of contractual detail
- approval by external agencies
- pre-implementation training
- implementation and data transfer from existing systems
- post-implementation review
- development of functionality after initial implementation.

2 Gain a high level of commitment from all stakeholders

It is beneficial to the procurement process for the organisation to be fully committed to the IM&T strategy and to the procurement route being undertaken. It was fundamental to the success of the project at Liverpool Women's Hospital that the Chief Executive and the Board of the Trust were aware not only of the overall strategic context and content of the project, but a high degree of detail of the procurement plan. The ability of the Chief Executive and non-executive directors to communicate effectively with their colleagues at Regional level is indicative of a strong organisational commitment to the development of the HISS and the use of PFI.

In dealing with the difficulties experienced at various times during procurement, the ability to field a team comprising of Trust management, clinicians and technicians was perceived by the approvers of the project as ample evidence of commitment to success.

3 Develop concurrent activities

There is substantial benefit in arranging the procurement plan over the shortest practicable timescale and to encourage concurrent activity on a number of fronts. This approach focuses the activities of the project team. The approach also requires a level of attention that precludes the side-tracking of key staff into other tasks. If the project plan is given sufficient high-level commitment and a tight timetable, much potential slippage can be avoided.

4 Develop risk and contingency plans

It is inevitable in any complex project that unforeseen events will occur. At the OBC stage it is necessary to produce a risk register and to place some indicative, but carefully reasoned, value upon risks. This evaluation of risk is developed through the FBC and included as a factor in the economic analysis of the proposal. An equally important use of the risk register and the evaluation of risk is in the management of that risk and the development of contingency plans in appropriate areas as required. Allocation of risk to the PFI contractor will protect the Trust, but there are areas of risk which are inappropriate or uneconomic to pass on in that way. Trusts must find ways of managing residual risks to protect them from undesirable outcomes.

Despite the best risk planning there are likely to be events during the course of the contract which are unforeseen. It is at these times that the benefit of proper risk planning comes into play. If foreseeable risks are planned for in the contract at an early stage, more effort and energy is available later to manage those events that are truly unforeseeable.

5 Develop ways of managing expectation

The involvement of senior clinical staff is an essential part of any successful HISS project. It is likely that the earliest contacts of the project team will be with the innovators and early adopters of new technology. These individuals will be keen to grasp the benefits that improved information systems will bring to their clinical practice. They are also likely to be individuals who are the most critical of delay in achieving what they see as valuable outcomes. It is an essential part of the HISS procurement plan that clinicians are educated on the benefits that the new system will bring, but at the same time given realistic expectations of timescales that are achievable.

Once the new systems are implemented, sufficient resource should be made available to develop them to meet the changing needs of clinicians. While it is likely that under a PFI contract the resources required for programming of system changes will be covered, it is a user requirement to draw up the new output specification. This requires both appropriate skills and time to enable the service provider to be properly informed of user requirements.

Once the new developments are put in place, time needs to be allowed to train users and to assist them in interpreting any new information that becomes available. These processes will inevitably cause delay between requests from users and the implementation of solutions to meet their needs. The process needs to be handled with care to maintain commitment and avoid frustration.

6 Developing effective relationships with PFI partners

The delivery of any service contract is dependent as much on the actions and attitudes of the people involved as the words within the document. Practical experience at Liverpool Women's Hospital has shown that while many eventualities have been covered by the PFI arrangements there are regularly events which push at the boundaries of the contract. It would be very simple for either party, and the service provider in particular, to draw demarcation lines based on the wording of the contract and beyond which they would not wish to move without further recompense.

The relationship between Liverpool Women's Hospital and Data General has developed through the quest to find practical solutions to

difficulties that have emerged during the procurement, contract negotiation and implementation phases. On a number of occasions there
have been trade-offs that have seen both parties giving ground in order
to develop both the long-term relationship and the system itself.
Examples of this include:

- the sacrifice of a number of desirable (but non-essential) outputs by
  the Trust in order to fund the development of an advanced data
  repository beyond the scope originally specified in the contract
- participation as a beta-testing site for UK software releases in return
  for a high degree of involvement in the specification of the new
  functionality being delivered
- comparison of this approach with other PFI sites where a more
  strictly contractual arrangement exists indicates that progress on
  whole system development is enhanced by the development of
  appropriately flexible arrangements with the PFI contractor.

7 Development of networks

Throughout the project it has become clear that there is great benefit
in the development of networks with other parties undergoing similar
work elsewhere. During the course of the project a diverse range of
networks has been formed. These have involved clinicians, managerial, technical and professional staff with other Trusts, IT suppliers
and associated organisations both in the UK and overseas. Contact
with these diverse organisations has brought its own benefit in giving
a wider view of opportunities across many aspects of the Trust's
work. These networks continue to develop and are increasingly
rewarding as the potential of IT and informatics becomes apparent
within the NHS.

Appendix A: Comparison of planned and actual timetables

Milestone	Original planned date	Revised planned date	Actual date	Comments
Initial registration			Nov 94	
Submit OBC	Sept 94	Nov 94	Dec 94	
OBC approved	Nov 94	Dec 94	Mar 95	
OJEC advertisement/ pre-qualification questionnaires	Jan 95	Feb 95	Apr 95	
Shortlist suppliers	Mar 95	Apr 95	Aug 95	
FBC to purchaser	Mar 95	Jun 95	Sept 95	
FBC to Region	Jun 95	Aug 95	Oct 95	
FBC to NHS Executive HQ	Jun 95	Sept 95	Nov 95	
Revised FBC to all parties	Jul 95	Oct 95	Feb 96	
FBC approval	Aug 95	Nov 95	Feb 96	
Invitation to tender	Aug 95	Dec 95	Mar 96	
PFI partner appointed	Sept 95	Jan 96	Apr 96	
Contract signed	Oct 95	Feb 96	Jul 96	
Phase 1 go live	June 96	Nov 96	Dec 96	
Phase 2 go live	Dec 96	Jul 97	Mar 97	
Phase 2a go live	Dec 96	Jul 97	Jul 97	
Phase 2b go live	Dec 96	Jul 97	Oct 97	
Upgrade to software version 4.6	May 98	May 98	May 98	
Phase 3 go live		Dec 97	Oct 98	

Appendix B: Evaluation of the responses to ITT

Technical evaluation

The ITT required additional information on the service proposed. These requirements provided the Trust with further information on the scope of the systems included within the contract, the method of the delivery of the service to the Trust, and the performance levels of the service.

In full, these information requirements were:

1 the range of future application software products included within the contract
2 the price of any known future application software products excluded from the contract price
3 the price of an on-site service team provided by the contractor
4 the technical configuration of the proposed service, including the interfacing to existing systems
5 the frequency of application software and central hardware upgrades
6 the provision of a disaster recovery service
7 the implementation project plans, defining the phased introduction of all modules
8 the quality management procedures employed by the contractor
9 the extent of the help-desk cover to be provided
10 the system performance and availability levels to be provided.

An evaluation matrix was drawn up by the HISS project board in advance of the tenders. Weights were agreed for each of the criteria.

CHAPTER NINE

Lessons learned and future directions

Roughly three years ago, the CBI published its influential report on *Private Skills in Public Service: tuning the PFI*. The subtitle of this report was very significant. The CBI went on to set out an agenda for how the initiative should be fine-tuned to improve its economy, efficiency and effectiveness. Much of this agenda was adopted by the new Labour administration and incorporated in the Bates' review which was subsequently commissioned. The policy has come a long way since then and has now taken firm root. It has the potential to achieve much more than what has been achieved to date.

This chapter pulls together some of the key lessons learned. It also considers what further steps could be taken to improve the PFI process and product. Finally, it concludes by considering the export potential of PFI to countries such as Jamaica, South Africa, New Zealand, Australia and Japan, where PFI can do much to rejuvenate ailing infrastructure and improve the delivery of public services which cannot be easily met by the public sector.

Key lessons

The evidence assembled in this book shows clearly that, notwithstanding its disappointing beginning, PFI can work. It is perfectly possible to develop and implement projects which meet the public and private sectors' minimum requirements:

- (for the public sector) to provide services which meet both the value-for-money and risk transfer tests
- (for the private sector) to achieve an investment opportunity which produces a reasonable return without unmanageable risks.

Lesson 1: A steep learning curve

PFI projects are inherently complex. Successful execution of such projects requires a multiplicity of core skills in areas such as corporate finance, law, economics, estates development and operation, information technology, facilities management and project management. Each of these areas in turn encompasses a range of topics. For example, in the case of law, the main topics include:

- arbitration and disputes resolution
- procurement regulations and contracts
- environment
- planning
- employment
- construction
- intellectual property
- public law
- taxation and VAT
- corporate law
- finance and security
- insurance (Morrison and Owen 1996).

Particular areas where lawyers have a role to play include:

- drafting of the notice for advertising the project in the relevant journal or source
- giving procurement advice
- drafting the various documentation (ITT, operating agreement, any lease or other agreements, etc.)
- giving advice on the impact of different terms and conditions
- providing legal due diligence work.

Financial advisers and economists are also a key group. Key roles here include:

- scoping and structuring the project
- preparing business case and investment appraisal
- advising on the construction of the public sector comparator
- preparing risk analysis
- defining the payment mechanism
- structuring the bid documentation
- advising on the evaluation criteria for assessing bids
- advising on the terms and conditions of the draft contract in the ITT

- financial evaluation of bids
- negotiations with bidders to contract award.

Technical advisers (engineers, surveyors, architects, etc.) are another key group. Their role is likely to include:

- helping to define the scope of the project in terms of services and desired outputs
- developing output specifications and measurement systems for the various services
- drafting the technical aspects of the advertisement for the project
- drafting the technical aspects of the ITT/ITN
- valuing assets that may be sold or included in the deal (e.g. surplus land)
- helping to value risks
- providing technical assumptions to be adopted in the business case/ investment appraisal
- providing advice on the technical aspects of monitoring the performance of the contractor.

Initially, much of this expertise will need to be bought in as the organisation seeks to progress up a steep learning curve. The strategy should be to minimise dependence on external expertise over time. Efforts should be made to procure these services cost-effectively. As noted before, the model adopted in the UK involved setting up PFUs in the key public sector departments, staffed by secondees from the private sector who have the requisite skills. To promote consistency across departments, the Treasury Task Force was established to develop central guidance, disseminate good practice, develop templates for specific types of transactions (e.g. standard contracts) to expedite the bidding process, and help departments to prioritise which projects should be taken forward under the PFI route.

Lesson 2: Consider 'PFIability' of projects

The UK experience has demonstrated that not all types of projects are suitable for PFI. To minimise abortive costs and waste of resources, the procuring entity should ensure the project will proceed before it is advertised. Once prioritised, the rate at which they are market tested should also be controlled. PFI projects must have the potential to create a win–win outcome for the public and private sectors. The type of projects which are likely to meet this requirement were discussed in Chapter 2 (*see* Box 2.6).

Lesson 3: Optimise risk allocation

To the detriment of value for money, the optimum allocation of risk has not always been achieved on a number of the earlier deals. As Wimpey Construction Investments Ltd (winner of the first PFI project in the education sector – University of Greenwich Avery Hill) put it, 'The public sector clients letting PFI schemes seem to be driven by the wish to score maximum points for risk transfer on each individual scheme, frequently forcing the private sector to take risks which are not within their control. They are not taking a long-term view of what is reasonable in order to ensure the long-term success of the programme' (House of Commons Treasury Committee 1996, p. 128).

In a similar vein, the CBI observed, 'There is still a tendency on the part of both the public and private sectors to "play tennis with a ball of risk"' (CBI 1996). For example, in the letting of the contracts for the first four DBFO road projects, volume risks were inappropriately shared with the private sector with the operator's income varying with road usage. Such an allocation is suboptimal because the private sector has no practical scope for encouraging traffic usage. The predictability of demand is also relevant to the allocation decision. The private sector is also hampered by the difficulties of forecasting traffic growth over long periods, hence difficulties in predicting their likely revenues over the 30-year life of the contract (NAO 1998). By contrast, in the first two prison projects, it was decided that demand risks should reside with the public sector since it is the Home Office and the courts who determine where offenders go. The payment mechanism in this case was thus based on availability of prison space rather than its usage.

This problem can be avoided in future by adopting the CBI's golden rules to guide the approach to risk allocation and management:

- value for money is maximised when risk is placed with the party who is best placed to manage it
- risk and control go together: the party to whom the risk is allocated must have freedom to determine how to manage it
- risk transfer must reflect what the market can absorb. This will vary over time as the private sector gains increased experience of managing the risks and executing PFI projects
- aim to share both rewards and risks to incentivise the private sector
- all risks should be identified, allocated and priced at the outset to allow flexibility throughout the project.

In addition to these golden rules, the type of project should be taken into account (i.e. financially free-standing, joint venture and DBFO). For example, usage risks may be appropriate to transfer under free-standing projects such as toll bridges or tunnels but the market is unlikely to accept payments based upon this currency for DBFO schemes.

As well as striving for optimal risk allocation, the public sector should also create incentives and opportunities for the private sector to bring substantial innovation and efficiency improvements to bear on the project. In the absence of these sources of efficiencies, it is unlikely that privately funded projects will provide better value for money than financing the same project with public money, given the higher cost of capital generally borne by the private sector compared to what the government faces in the market for gilt-edged stock.

Lesson 4: Avoid reinventing the wheel

PFI lessons have been learned the hard way, often at considerable cost to both the public and private sector. Anything which lessens the length of the procurement process will help to expedite these projects and reduce the associated transaction costs. The UK experience has underlined:

- the need for standardisation where appropriate (e.g. contract clauses, OJEC advertisement, standard procedure for obtaining information from tenderers, etc.)
- development of clear rules for guiding the policy
- development of up-to-date guidance
- the need to ensure the legal apparatus is in place to provide the necessary safeguards to financiers and the private sector in general
- the need to batch smaller schemes together to make them commercially viable
- the need to scope projects optimally with a focus on outputs and services.

Wherever possible, it is also important to delay the more expensive elements of the bid costs (e.g. full design, obtaining firm funding commitments from financiers, etc.) until the number of bidders has been reduced. This would help to reduce the cost of the bidding process. Bidding costs to one consortium have been known to exceed £4m on a contract with an expected net present cost of £232m (NAO 1998, p. 25). The further in the bidding process a bidder progresses, the higher the costs he faces. In the case of this particular bidder, costs incurred up to the pre-qualification stage were under £100 000, rising to up to £2m up to the shortlisting stage and over £4m up to the reserve/winning bidder stage.

Lesson 5: The importance of competition

There is evidence that the process of shortlisting bidders and selecting the preferred partner was not always conducted in a manner consistent with maintaining acute competition and obtaining best value for money. This is clearly evidenced in the various NAO reviews of the early PFI deals in transport, prisons and health. For example, the NAO observed that the consortia shortlisted to bid for each of the first four DBFO road projects were not always the most suitable ones. This was because of the additional criterion which the Highways Agency built into the selection process, namely, 'to spread the work around to sustain private sector interest and thus assist in meeting the objective of creating a private sector road operating industry' (NAO 1998, p. 13).

Partly for the same reason, the Prison Service decided against letting the Bridgend and Fazakerley contracts to the same bidder, Securicor/Costain, even though they submitted the most competitive bid. 'The Service decided to award only one contract (Bridgend) to Securicor/Costain, and the other (Fazakerley) to Group 4/Tarmac even though Group 4/Tarmac's proposal was £31m higher for that contract, and Securicor/Costain had said they could offer further cost reductions if they were awarded both contracts' (NAO 1998, p. viii). Although both projects generated aggregate savings of 10% compared to the public sector comparators, virtually all these savings resulted from the Bridgend contract.

Lesson 6: Overstating benefits of the PFI solution and distorting the PSC

Considerable care needs to be taken in assessing the costs, benefits and risks associated with the shortlisted options, particularly the selection of the preferred method for funding the project. Again, the NAO reviews are instructive in this regard. They found evidence of inappropriate public sector comparators, spurious risk analysis, double-counting of benefits, including nominal with real values in discounted cashflow analyses, inappropriate discount rates and inadequate sensitivity analysis. For example, savings from the first four DBFO roads were overstated by £69m as a result of using the wrong discount rate – 8% instead of 6% (NAO 1998, p. 4).

The widely held belief in the early days that PFI is the 'only game in town' may well have created perverse incentives for departments and their advisers to distort the results of the economic appraisals. The steep learning curve associated with the policy, coupled with the lack of published guidance, would, doubtless, have contributed to these technical weaknesses. For example, definitive guidance on public sector comparators and risk analysis is not expected to be published before late 1999.

Further improvements to the PFI process and product

This section considers what further improvements may be made to the PFI process and product. Many of the reforms introduced since May 1997, particularly those heralded in the Bates' review, have been aimed at improving the PFI process rather than the product. As a result, they focused on issues such as production of guidance, provision of training, prioritisation of projects and involvement of key stakeholders in the planning of schemes. These process improvements are reflected in Box 2.4, which summarises the key recommendations from the Department of Health's PFI review.

The latest list of published schemes with Treasury Task Force approval demonstrates the diversity and extent of penetration of PFI in the delivery of public services. The challenge now is to find more direct ways of improving the PFI *product* and deepening the involvement of the private sector in the various parts of the public sector. These reforms should be aimed at improving value for money from such transactions and enhancing the quantity and quality of services offered to the public. This issue needs to be considered on a sector-by-sector basis. Further, systematic research should be undertaken to identify good practices from across the public sector and make them widely available in the form of guidance. At the time of writing (June 1999), the conclusions from the second Bates' review are not available. It is likely that this review will focus on improvements to the PFI product.

New models of PFI/PPP

In the quest for improved value for money, consideration should be given to all possible variants on PFI/different models of PPP when there is demonstrable evidence that deviations from the classic model is the only feasible approach. For example, within the health sector, the *mixed funding* option has been adopted in several projects as this was the only way to achieve a viable, affordable and value-for-money outcome. This model was first pioneered by South Manchester University Hospital Trust. In its review of the first two PFI contracts in the prisons sector, the NAO noted '. . . the Service could have considered awarding separate building and operating contracts which they have previously been able to use effectively with good savings' (NAO 1997).

One is reminded of the maxim which was frequently associated with the policy in its early years, 'deals not rules'. In the context of other potential models of PFI/PPP, this boils down to proceeding with the deal which gives the best value for money to the public sector in the particular circumstance. This suggests a need for flexibility on the part of all those who are responsible for vetting business cases, including the NAO. The NAO have made clear that '. . . they will not wish to criticise departments simply because they have departed from tradition and innovated. We recognise that innovation must involve taking risks, but welcome well-thought out innovation and risk taking' (cited in House of Commons Treasury Committee 1996, p. 132).

Intra- and inter-sectoral procurements

The feasibility of batch procurements should be considered. This could include projects within the same sector (e.g. two neighbouring NHS trusts undertaking a single procurement to meet their respective service needs). It could also transcend sectoral boundaries (e.g. joint procurements could be undertaken between, say, education, prisons and health). This could be approached along the lines of 'joined-up procurement planning', based on the Health Action or Education Action Zone principle. Although much more complex and difficult to scope and manage, this should, in principle, result in lower procurement costs for the public sector and, if properly scoped, improved value for money from sources such as additional income-generating activities from third parties, scope for additional uses of the asset created, using information technology to re-engineer business processes and potential to exploit surplus assets (particularly land).

Value for money may be further enhanced if the procurement is undertaken by a single entity on behalf of the project sponsors. One option may be to establish a procurement authority expressly for this purpose. The remit of this authority could extend beyond providing procurement services to encompassing other services such as providing an advisory service (financial, legal and technical), alternative funding and contract management services. In terms of its staffing and working arrangements, this could be modelled along the lines of the Treasury Task Force. Otherwise, the full benefits are unlikely to result on account of skills constraints. There is already evidence that the private sector has begun to reorganise itself to exploit the opportunity presented by PFI/PPP. Strategic alliances are being formed between and within constructors, service providers, financiers, advisers and the other key players involved in such transactions. The public sector also needs to devise efficient and effective organisational vehicles to take the policy forward.

If the synergies from these partnerships are realised, it should produce a win–win outcome for both the public and private sector. A climate must be created to provide incentives to both parties to make best use of taxpayers' money. This argument for the creation of long-term, multi-faceted, PFI/PPP 'mission-focused' organisations is developed further by Hope (1998) in his thought-provoking article on *PFI plc: a route to partnership and prosperity*. Hope contends, with much justification, that PFI plc can deliver further benefits for both parties:

> A long-term investment-led PFI plc approach has real benefits for all. The end user customer gets improved service delivery, better value for money and increased innovation. It also reduces the overhead for non-core services. For the staff transferred into a private sector organisation, there are opportunities to further career development. For the private sector . . . there are commercial gains to be had, especially if decisions are not based on a need to satisfy third party financiers' (pp. 51–2).

Such multi-agency investment should also take into account the importance of 'location'. In some cases this may act as a constraint, depending on the nature of the service. It is possible for PFI to deliver good value for money in respect of a service in one location and poor value for money for the same service in another location. This could result from differences in market conditions and risks.

Better management of risks and a cheaper source of financing

The lessons learned over the past seven years about risk management should be used to guide future deals. One would expect both parties (i.e. the public and private sectors) to learn a lot about the risks which apply to various projects, particularly about their potential impact and likelihood. Economic theory would suggest that future deals should benefit from a lower risk premium since the private sector ought to be more familiar with managing the risks in question and gaining better information about wider managerial and organisational risks associated with various public sector bodies. Their ability to manage the risks, both the likelihood and the financial impact, should improve value for money to the public sector.

Another source of improved value for money and affordability should result from the favourable developments in the money market. Interest rates are now on a downward trend. This trend is not a short-term aberration. It is a direct result of the success of the government's economic policy and the European Monetary Union's commitment to low inflation and sustainable economic growth.

At the same time, there is growing competition between financiers which is exerting downward pressure on the cost of capital. For example, unlike the early years of PFI, project/bank finance is now moving towards longer maturities to eliminate one of the main advantages from bond/capital markets finance. For many of the early deals, the maturity period for bank loans was typically 21 years compared to 30 years for bond finance. This created affordability problems for many schemes, rendering bank finance relatively unattractive, notwithstanding its other advantages. As the PFI market has matured, this gap in the maturity of finance raised from both of these sources has narrowed. Credit margins have also reduced. Bank deals with 30-year maturities are likely to be commonplace before long. This is a clear testament that the market is now comfortable with the types of risk inherent in PFI transactions.

Better scoped deals, a better equipped public sector, a competitive procurement process for the facility and services underlying the output specification, more funding options and greater competitive pressure in the money market, better understanding of how to allocate and manage the risks associated with PFI procurements, and more effective partnership arrangements between and within the public and private sectors should lead to further improvements in value for money to the taxpayer. These are all important aspects of the PFI product which, if approached properly, can cumulatively produce a huge impact on value for money.

Monitoring long-term revenue consequences

One process improvement which deserves greater prominence is the need for public sector bodies to develop effective mechanisms to monitor the long-term revenue consequences of PFI/PPP projects. As we have seen, PFI converts capital expenditure into current expenditure in the form of long-term service contracts with private sector bodies. Apart from passing on the cost of the investment to future years, once these contracts are entered into, it is difficult to get out of them without incurring considerable cost. This raises important issues of inter-generational equity and public expenditure control. Things have moved on since HM Treasury reported in 1996 to the Treasury Committee:

> So far as the Private Finance Unit in the Treasury is concerned, it does not have a role. It is even more remote than, say, the NHS Executive from trusts in relation to the monitoring of obligations that are entered into or are anticipated as being entered into by trusts . . . it is very much the responsibility of departments and they are the ones that are informed as to the arrangements that they are entering into for monitoring those commitments, and some of these are as small as a few hundred thousand pounds' (House of Commons Treasury Committee 1996, p. xi).

Systematic arrangements are now in place in a number of Departments to monitor forward commitments arising from such transactions. The Department of Health provides an example of best practice. Its PFI revenue consequences model is designed to answer questions such as: what are the revenue implications of all PFI schemes approved in the NHS to date in a particular year or over the primary period of the contract? How would revenue expenditure change with different levels of PFI approvals in a given year (say £1 billion of new deals in 2004)? What effect would changes in the key underlying variables (e.g. cost of capital, maturity period for the loan, the capital to services ratio, budget constraint, etc.) have on revenue consequences?

As better information becomes available from monitoring, evaluation and learning, these models and their underlying assumptions should be continuously updated and refined. Then, and only then, will the information produced contribute meaningfully to the control of public expenditure – a key cornerstone of Government economic policy. At the same time, the public should take a greater interest in the costs and benefits of long-term PFI/PPP contracts. This will provide greater incentive to monitor and evaluate the contracts.

PFI within an international context

PFI is generally relevant in situations where achievement of the public sector's objectives relies on buildings, infrastructure or any other form of capital spending. The policy has begun to attract considerable interest from overseas governments and international organisations. This presents a major opportunity for UK companies and advisers to capitalise on their PFI experience in the global economy.

This would not be the first time the UK has exported public sector policies. Indeed, the UK has been at the forefront in pioneering policies to improve the delivery of public services by forming partnerships with the private sector. As noted in Chapter 1, related programmes such as privatisation, market testing and outsourcing were all developed or perfected in the UK. All of these policies have since been exported. For example, our success with privatising state monopolies has been successfully adopted in many other countries. More recently, privatisation is being vigorously pursued in the former communist countries in Eastern Europe.

Now that PFI has taken firm root in the UK, this success is likely to be repeated elsewhere. Bill Davidson, director of PFI Scotland at KPMG, listed the following countries among those who are keen to adopt and adapt the policy:

- Scandinavian countries – Finland already has one DBFO PFI road and a number of other projects in the pipeline.
- Other European countries – a major PFI project is underway in Berlin for a new airport and a tunnel project is proposed in Leipzig. Spain also has several road projects. Switzerland, Italy and France have all expressed interest in the policy.
- Asia – Japan has considered the policy 'in great detail' and 'I would expect them to adopt the principles' (Davidson 1988, p. 72).
- Australia – there are several PFI hospital projects underway in Australia. This is expected to be a big market for PFI.
- New Zealand – is currently considering applying the policy, particularly in the fields of DBFO roads and hospitals.
- Africa – there are a couple of PFI-type projects already underway in South Africa. 'South Africa has an almost limitless need for investment in all aspects of traditional public services such as health, water and sewerage, transport, prisons, education and so on. Indeed, in some areas, it is difficult to decide where to start as the need is so

great and the potential benefits to South Africans a veritable quantum leap' (p. 72).
- USA, Latin America and the Caribbean – Davidson (1988) did not report on this zone. However, discussions with a senior official at the IMF indicate there is potential interest in these countries once they grasp the principles of what is involved and become aware of the potential benefits to the public sector. For example, there are, indeed, considerable opportunities in Jamaica for PFI-type projects in areas such as transport (DBFO roads, railway lines, hospitals, schools, prisons, police stations, office accommodation, etc.).

If effective PFI or public–private partnerships are to develop in such countries without incurring unnecessary costs and delays, the UK experience demonstrates that the public and private sectors must address the following issues early in the process.

The public sector must:

- consider whether the project is suited to PFI and set a *de minimis* level for such projects given the exorbitant procurement costs associated with 'small' schemes
- demonstrate commitment to the PFI procurement process and make timely decisions
- establish an effective project team with all the requisite skills from the outset of the project or develop a strategy for gaining access to the relevant skills
- specify its requirements clearly with emphasis on desired outputs and outcomes and allow the private sector maximum flexibility to meet its requirements
- possess the legal power to enter into the proposed contract
- be able to afford the cost of the scheme year on year and over the duration of the contract
- identify risks properly and adopt a realistic approach to risk allocation
- provide clear guidance to support delivery of the policy
- develop standard documents and contract clauses where possible to minimise the procurement costs
- take steps to allay the private sector's fears (particularly financiers) of complying with a new policy, e.g. by enacting legislations to introduce the policy and remove all doubts
- ensure open and fair procurements are undertaken and that the preferred partner satisfies all the requirements of the policy, particularly those relating to risk transfer and value for money
- ensure the market has the capacity to deliver its service requirements (suppliers, financiers, advisers etc.).

The private sector must:

- understand the objectives of the public sector and the constraints under which it operates
- establish an effective team to drive the project
- ensure the consortium which it puts in place has the necessary skills and experience to meet the public sector's service requirements
- have access to the capital needed to fund the project on terms which make the project affordable to the public sector at the same time as meeting the value-for-money requirements – this may require financiers to offer project finance over longer maturity periods than the current norm
- adopt a realistic approach to negotiating all aspects of the contract, including risks and the desired rate of return on their investment
- offer innovative solutions to meeting the public sector's requirements.

The partners to the transaction must develop an effective working relationship, based on mutual trust and recognition of each other's corporate objectives. *Long-term partnerships* spanning up to 30 years require time, energy and effort to maintain momentum and to meet contractual obligations without resort to litigation and other heavy-handed measures.

Conclusion

The PFI/PPP path has now been well trodden, even in the local authority sector where the initiative was particularly slow to take root. The UK's experience confirms Bates' conclusion 'when handled well, the PFI can work to the mutual advantage of users of public services, taxpayers and companies seeking new business opportunities'. Like the Industrial Revolution, 'late-comers' can learn a great deal from the UK's experience with PFI – a major policy breakthrough by any standard. They can skip stages and learn valuable lessons from our experience. The challenge to potential UK PFI exporters is to prioritise the countries of interest. As with all decision making, considerations about costs, benefits and risks of the various options will determine the actual choice and its timing.

References

Accounting Standards Board (1998) *Amendment to FRS5 'Reporting the Substance of Transactions: Private Finance Initiative and similar contracts'*. ASB, London.

Arnold G (1988) *Corporate Finance Management*. Financial Times/Pitman, London.

Audit Commission (1998) *Taking the Initiative: a framework for purchasing under the private finance initiative*. Audit Commission, London.

Central IT Unit (1998) *Private Finance and IT: a practical guide*. Cabinet Office in HM Treasury, London.

CIPFA (1997) *The Private Finance Initiative: accounting and auditing issues*. CIPFA, London.

Cirell S, Bennett J, Hann R (1997) *The Private Finance Initiative and Local Government*, vols 1 and 2. FT Law and Tax, London.

Confederation of British Industry (1996) *Private Skills in Public Service: tuning the Private Finance Initiative*. CBI, London.

Corry D (ed) (1997) *Public Expenditure: effective management and control*. Dryden Press, London.

Davidson B (1998) Best of British. *Private Finance Initiative Journal*. **3**(1): 71–3.

Department of Health (1997) *The New NHS: modern, dependable*. The Stationery Office, London.

Department of Health (1998) *A First Class Service: quality in the new NHS*. DoH, London.

Department of Health (1998) *Our Healthier Nation: a contract for health*. The Stationery Office, London.

Dix A (1999) Private eye. *Health Service Journal*. **109**(5639): 9–12.

Flanagan R, Norman G (1983) *Risk Management and Construction*. Blackwell Science, Oxford.

Gaffney D, Pollock A (1997) *Can the NHS Afford the Private Finance Initiative?* Health Policy and Economic Research Unit, London.

Hope J (1998) PFI plc: a route to 'partnership and prosperity'. *Private Finance Initiative Journal*. **3**(1).

Heald D (1996) *The Private Finance Initiative: value for money and public expenditure control.* House of Commons Treasury Committee, pp. 160–9.

HM Prison and Private Finance Panel (1996) *The Procurement of Custodial Services at Bridgend and Fazakerley.* HM Treasury, London.

HM Treasury (1991) *Economic Appraisal in Central Government: a technical guide for government departments.* HMSO, London.

HM Treasury (1995) *Private Opportunity, Public Benefit.* HM Treasury, London.

HM Treasury (1997) *Appraisal and Evaluation in Central Governmnt.* The Stationery Office, London.

House of Commons Treasury Committee (1996) *Session 1995–96: Sixth Report on the Private Finance Initiative.* The Stationery Office, London.

Klein M (1997) The risk premium for evaluating public projects. *Oxford Review of Economic Policy.* **13**(4): 29–42.

KPMG and The Major Contractors Group (1998) *The Benefits of PFI.* KPMG, London.

Lumby S (1995) *Investment Appraisal and Financial Decisions.* Chapman & Hall, London.

Manning K (1996) *Delivering PFI Healthcare Solutions.* Newchurch Consulting, London.

Meara R (1997) *Building Services and Servicing Buildings: the Private Finance Initiative in the NHS.* Institute of Health Services Management, London.

Moran K (1997) *Investment Appraisal for Non-Financial Managers.* Pitman Publishing, London.

Morrison N, Owen N (1996) *Private Finance Initiative.* FT Law and Tax, London.

Nash P and Manning K (1995) Testing private finance in the NHS. *British Journal of Healthcare Management.* **1**: 9.

National Audit Office (1997) *Report on the PFI Contracts for Bridgend and Fazakerley Prisons.* NAO, London.

National Audit Office (1998) *The Private Finance Initiative: the first four design, build, finance and operate road contracts.* NAO, London.

National Health Service Executive (1992) *Getting Better with Information.* NHSE, Leeds.

National Health Service Executive (1995) *Private Finance and Capital Investment Projects,* HSG(95)15. NHSE, Leeds.

National Health Service Executive (1994) *Capital Investment Manual*. The Stationery Office, London.

National Health Service Executive (1997) *The Purpose, Organisation, Management and Funding of the NHS: a guide for the private sector*. NHSE, Leeds.

National Health Service Executive (1998) *Information for Health*. NHSE, Leeds.

National Health Service Executive (1999) *Capital Investment Manual*. NHSE, Leeds (in press).

National Health Service Executive (1999) *PFI Manual*. NHSE, Leeds (in press).

National Health Service Executive (1999) *Public–Private Partnerships in the NHS: the private finance initiative*. NHSE, Leeds (in press).

National Health Service (Residual Liabilities) Act (1996) The Stationery Office, London.

Oxford Economic Research Associates Ltd (1996) *Infrastructure in the UK: public projects and private money*. Oxera Press, Oxford.

Private Finance Panel (May 1996) *5 Steps to the Appointment of Advisers to PFI Projects*. HM Treasury, London.

Private Finance Panel (October 1996) *Writing an Output Specification*. HM Treasury, London.

Royal Fine Art Commission (1997) *Design Quality and the Private Finance Initiative*. Thomas Telford, London.

Terry F (1996) The Private Finance Initiative – overdue reform or policy breakthrough? *Journal of Public Money and Management*. **16**(1): 9–16.

Treasury Task Force (September 1997) PFI Technical Note No. 1: *How to Account for PFI Transactions*. HM Treasury, London.

Treasury Task Force (November 1997) *Partnerships for Prosperity*. HM Treasury, London.

Treasury Task Force (March 1998) Policy Statement No. 2: *Public Sector Comparators and Value for Money*. HM Treasury, London.

Treasury Task Force (April 1998) *A Step-by-Step Guide to the PFI Procurement Process*. HM Treasury, London.

Treasury Task Force (May 1998) PFI Technical Note No. 2: *How to Follow EC Procurement Procedure and Advertise in the OJEC*. HM Treasury, London.

Treasury Task Force (January 1999) *Standardisation of PFI Contracts*. HM Treasury, London.

Further reading

Dunningham M, Gaffney, D, Majeed F *et al.* (1997) What happens when the private sector plans hospital services for the NHS: three case studies under the Private Finance Initiative. *British Medical Journal.* **314**(7089): 1266–71.

Grout P (1997) The economics of the Private Finance Initiative. *Oxford Review of Economic Policy.* **13**(4): 53–66.

Private Finance Panel (April 1996) *Guidelines for Smoothing the Procurement Process.* HM Treasury, London.

Private Finance Panel (May 1996) *Risk and Reward in PFI Contracts.* HM Treasury, London.

Private Finance Panel (October 1996) *Transferability of Equity.* HM Treasury, London.

Private Finance Panel (October 1996) *Basic Contractual Terms.* HM Treasury, London.

Private Finance Panel (October 1996) *PFI in Government Accommodation.* HM Treasury, London.

Private Finance Panel (January 1997) *Further Contractual Issues.* HM Treasury, London.

Private Finance Panel (March 1997) *VAT on PFI Service Projects.* HM Treasury, London.

Royal Institution of Chartered Surveyors (1996) *The Private Finance Initiative: the essential guide.* RICS Business Services, London.

Treasury Task Force (October 1997) Policy Statement No. 1: *PFI and Public Expenditure Allocations.* HM Treasury, London.

Treasury Task Force (August 1998) Policy Statement No. 3: *PFI and Public Expenditure Allocations for Non-Departmental Public Bodies.* HM Treasury, London.

Treasury Task Force (October 1998) Policy Statement No. 4: *Disclosure of Information and Consultation with Staff and other Interested Parties.* HM Treasury, London.

Treasury Task Force (September 1998) PFI Technical Note No. 3: *How to Appoint and Manage Advisers*. HM Treasury, London.

Treasury Task Force (1999) PFI Technical Note No. 4: *How to Construct a Public Sector Comparator*. HM Treasury, London (in press).

Index

risk by type of *83*
control risk
  allocation 81
  meaning 66
conventional procurement method, PFI versus
  4–6, *5*
Conventionally Funded Options (CFO) 102
cost of capital, public and private sectors 11
costs
  build cost *see* build cost
  capital *see* capital costs
  equipment, value for money analyses 95
  equivalent annual cost (EAC) 103, *104*
  identification and quantification, value for
    money 94–5
  legal, Calderdale hospital project 135
  net present cost (NPC) 103, *104*
  non-financial, assessments 103
  operating cost risk *see* operating cost risk
  revenue, value for money 95
  spread 10
  works, value for money analyses 95
CPAG *see* Capital Prioritisation Advisory
  Group

Dartford River Crossing 8
design, build, finance, operate (DBFO) schemes
  6, 8
  health service, adaptation to 31
design risk
  allocation 77–8
  meaning 65
detailed statements of needs (DSON)
  Liverpool Women's Hospital IS/IT project
    155
development agreements 41
development risk *see* construction and
  development risk
discounted cash flows, value for money
  comparisons 103
dissolution of NHS trusts, residual liabilities
  29
Dockland Light Railway Extension 8
Dorrel, Stephen 13
DSON *see* detailed statements of needs

EAC (equivalent annual cost) 103, *104*
economic advantage, contract award basis 56
economic appraisal
  Calderdale hospital project 130
  value for money comparisons 103
economic case 114–15
economies of scale 9
economists' roles 184–5
efficiency, commercial incentives for 9
employment issues, Calderdale hospital project
  137
equipment
  costs, value for money analyses 95
  strategy 117–8
equity providers 6
equivalent annual cost (EAC) 103, *104*

evaluation criteria 56
  Liverpool Women's Hospital IS/IT project
    164, 181
  see also scoring systems
evaluation model, Calderdale hospital project
  127–8
executive agencies 1
expectation management, Liverpool Women's
  Hospital IS/IT project 178
expertise within public sector 16
external advisers 38

favourable PFI project characteristics *36*
FBC *see* Full Business Cases
financial advisers' roles 184–5
financial case 115
financial close 58–9
financial issues, Calderdale hospital project 138
financially free standing projects 6, 8
financiers 6
  Calderdale hospital project 133
  fears of 27–8, 29
  involvement in bid process 57–8
  Liverpool Women's Hospital IS/IT project
    168
  risk analysis 64–5
financing, cheaper sources 191–2
force majeure events 68–9
  Calderdale hospital project 137
Full Business Cases (FBC) 32, 34, 109
  approval
    criteria 111–12
    thresholds *110*
  Calderdale hospital project 130–2
  commercial case 115–16
  economic case 114–15
  equipment strategy 117–8
  information technology issues 117
  financial case 115
  Liverpool Women's Hospital IS/IT project
    162, 165–7
  project management case 116–17
  purpose 110–11
  strategic case 113–14
  structure 113
  submitting to NHSE and Treasury 59
  timetable 117
  value for money tests 99
future improvements 189
  financing, cheaper sources 191–2
  intra- and inter-sectoral procurements 190–1
  long-term revenue consequences monitoring
    193
  new models of PFI/PPP 189–90
  risk management improvements 191–2

GIGO principle (garbage in, garbage out) 70
'gold-plating' 10
guarantees 41

headleases 41
health authority role